Life's
a
Mango

Jen Compton acknowledges the Australian Aboriginal and Torres Strait Islander peoples of this nation. She acknowledges the Turrbal Aboriginal Nation, the traditional custodians of the land on which her book was written and published. She pays her respects to ancestors and Elders, past and present. Jen Compton is committed to honouring Australian Aboriginal and Torres Strait Islander peoples' unique cultural and spiritual relationships to the land, waters and seas and their rich contribution to society.

Life's a Mango: A Guide to Awakening through Mindful Rhyming Wisdom
© Jen Compton 2021

ISBN: 978-1-925833-85-0 (Paperback)
       978-1-925833-86-7 (eBook)

A catalogue record for this work is available from the National Library of Australia

Cover Design: Wally Martin
Mandala Design: Inha Semiankova
Internal Illustrations: Brooke Dobbie
Design and Typeset: Wally Martin and Ocean Reeve Publishing
Printed in Australia by Ocean Reeve Publishing
www.oceanreeve.com

Published by Jen Compton and Ocean Reeve Publishing
www.oceanreevepublishing.com

Life's a Mango

A Guide to Awakening through Mindful Rhyming Wisdom

Jen Compton

Praise for Life's a Mango

Jen offers inspiring wisdom in directing us how to find joy the only place it abides – the here and now.

David Michie
author of *The Dalai Lama's Cat* series and *Buddhism for Busy People*

The wisdom found here is deep, is profound and takes one to the core of existence where contribution to self and others adds meaning to life. Self-compassion reaches to others once one gives. This is captured in each of these superb poems. Live by these poems and you will live peacefully.

John Hendry, 0AM

Thank you for your verses, they make my heart sing. They're a shield against curses that a hard day can bring. Your sound advice and your comforting rhymes make me think twice before grudging tough times. Your wisdom and insight are a gift to all and a guiding light when we stumble and fall. I'm grateful for your book and your attitude to life. You provide a deeper look and a way out of strife.

Dr Helena Popovic
MBBS, medical doctor, best-selling author and conference speaker

I find *Life's a Mango* a clever and gentle nudge into thoughtfulness through persuasive rhyme … ahh

Julie Borgelt
architect

This little book is packed with thought provoking poems, is calming and reflects on life. We as a congregation have used it on numerous occasions as "The Thought for the Day" during our church services. All in all an excellent read.

Dr John M Ballany
Session Clerk, Carnbee Church of Scotland, Carnbee, Fife

Jen provides us with the power of POW in this juicy little book. Packed full of magical rhyming gems of the joy of BEING that were inspired not just by Tolle and the Dharma but by her own life experiences. This book contains a wealth of wonderful wisdom that can be life-changing but it has the exciting bonus of being FUN to read either to yourself or aloud with friends. Everyone can learn how to **Be** a more joyful and compassionate person by applying the "Magic of the Mango" in their daily life.

Graham Malcolm
science teacher

Jen is a veritable Dr. Seuss.

Michele Pinney
teacher

I love the timeless gems of wisdom that are portrayed in a witty and easy to identify with way. People of all ages will laugh and be touched by this beautiful, uplifting book. I also love how there are mandalas to colour and blank pages for journaling. My son and I sometimes read a poem before heading out for the day, which helps us breathe, laugh and be thankful. My favourite poem is *Thank you ABC* which helps me slow down and remember the many gifts in my life.

Cielle Van Vuuren
artist & mother

I love that when I read Jen's poems they feel like they were written for me. They speak to my soul and make me truly think about my life.

Jodi Cross
teacher

Jen exudes positivity and this shines through in her verse. It is an *everyman's* guide to getting the most out of daily living, warts and all.

Enid Eyles
retired deputy principal

Jen is a remarkable, beautiful person and poet. She is able to capture in words the beauty and nature that come from the heart. It's an absolute privilege to hear her reciting her poems and just to immerse myself in her creativity. She's a master of verse and art all in one.

Tom Stodulka
mediator and poet

Jen Compton's poetic advice is simple but profound, just as all universal truths are.

Robina Courtin
subject of the documentary *Chasing Buddha*

This book of inspirations conjures pictures and feelings of joy for the past and excitement for the possibilities of the future. Each inspiration soothes the soul, healing the child and adult within.

Vicki Bennett
author of *The Book of Hope – Antidote for Anxiety*

I like *Who Am I* because it's just plain catchy and it was easy to remember. When I said the poem, the words made me feel calm and relaxed.

Hayden
aged 11

Life's a Mango is beautifully written and uplifting. When I got the book I was asked to open it randomly. The poem I got was *Your Heart*. It could not have been more perfect for how I was feeling at the time. A must-have book when in need of love and wisdom.

Antonella
social worker

For those who search for a truly humane, compassionate, respectful way of living, Jen Compton's book, *Life's a Mango*, is just the book for you. With her humorous, direct, simple and light touch she offers through her verse, a personal and thought-provoking perspective on many aspects of everyday life. All those little moments in our daily routines become topics for her verse and give cause to pause and reflect on who we are and who we would like to be.

Peter Cooper
retired school principal

I like this book because it reminds me about being present in the moment. It's positive. I like its positive-ness. It helps me relax at the end of a long day.

Sophia
aged 10

You are such an inspirational lady. I love your book. Congratulations. It's beautiful inside and out. I wish you all the success in the future. I think you are so clever to have captured the secret to happiness so simply in your poems. I will keep your book close to hand and recommend it to everyone I know. Everyone would be more at peace if they read your lovely book.

Simone Feiler
Brisbane Audiobook Production

For Mum and Dad

You've travelled with me
Every step of the way.
Your love and support
Helped make me today.

You've always been there,
Through thick and through thin.
Wherever I am,
My rock you have been.

Thank you so much
For all that you've done.
I picked the best parents.
With you two, I won!

For Nana and Papa

There was nowhere on earth
I felt more myself than with you.
Like a soft warm blanket,
Your love was gentle and true.

I was relaxed with you both.
I could just **be** me.
Your smiles, hugs and cuddles
Used to fill me with glee.

Thank you for teaching me
How to smile and be kind.
Your love lives on in my heart.
Without it, I'd be blind.

You showed me the way
To live simply and just be.
We cooked, walked, played cards,
You sure did care for me.

Whenever I saw you,
My heart jumped for joy.
You always brought me a gift,
Some token or toy.

I wish I had asked you
Much more of your past.
Your life as a young person,
I guess it all went so fast.

We always remember those
Whom to us have been kind.
I'll never forget you.
Your love for me was divine.

When I read Andrew Bienkowski's book, *Radical Gratitude,* I was deeply moved. I contacted him and we started exchanging letters via snail mail. I really wanted to meet this person! Trusting my heart, I flew to Buffalo, New York. It was an honour and a joy to connect with Andy and his family. They are now my friends.

This photo was taken on the day Andy and his son, Tim, took me to visit Niagara Falls.

> *I am not the slave of my past, but the master of my future. Whatever situation I am in is a result of decisions and choices I have made. I am continuously creating my reality with my thoughts and my decisions. Everything I do, think, feel and decide now is creating the reality in which I will live in the future.*
>
> **Andrew Bienkowski**

Foreword

Poetry is the music of the soul. Jen Compton's poetry is like a collection of beautiful songs that gives voice to the spiritual reality of our lives. Its simplicity, sweetness and rhythm will expose you to the wisdom that will feed your soul.

When Jen asked me if I would write the foreword to her book, *Life's a Mango*, I was delighted to say yes. Poets are my heroes and her poetry with the emphasis on living in the now reminds me of Rumi, Hafiz and Eckhart Tolle who have always been my heroes.

Jen's poetry has the power to inspire you and change the direction of your life. It will bring a smile to your face and will make your life more meaningful in this world of uncertainty and complexity.

Use this book as a guide on your inner journey; as a prism through which you will discover some very important universal truths about nature, ego, suffering, love, gratitude, intimacy and much more.

Above all, Jen Compton's rhymes will bring you joy. They will bring you healing if you need it. To get the full benefit of this book, read only one poem a day. Then think about it. Let it sink in. Reflect. Let it affect you.

Andrew Bienkowski
retired psychologist and co-author of *Radical Gratitude* and *One Life to Give*

How to use this book

Hello friend. Welcome to *Life's a Mango*. Since the first edition was published, readers tell me that each day they enjoy opening the book randomly and seeing which poem the universe has chosen for them at this moment. Many like to whisper the words, *May I be guided by love,* whilst they close their eyes and open the book. It's curious, they say, as to how the message contained in the poem is often just what they needed to hear.

Of course, you can also use the contents page as a guide where you will find a description of each poem. The poems have been divided into four sections according to the nature of their content. Parts of the mango have been used as metaphors for the sections – The Skin, The Brown Bits, The Flesh and The Seed.

At the back of the book, you'll find mandalas to colour in as well as blank journal pages where you may like to write or draw your reflections of the poems. Reading the poems out loud is very powerful and as many of my students have discovered, learning the poems off by heart turns them into something very personal. Your live recitals are sure to delight family and friends and if you need some inspiration, you can see me reciting some of the poems on my website, jencompton.com. I wrote the poem, *A Love Journey,* as a gift to my mum for her 80th birthday. Friends of mine have borrowed this poem, as well as others, and adapted them to suit their audience. I find this both exciting and inspiring.

Just as you add colour to life, so too can you add colour and character to this book by colouring the trees, illustrations and the mandalas.

May your daily guide to awakening through mindful rhyming wisdom, *Life's a Mango,* **be** transformed into something very personal, just for you.

Take care. Stay safe.

Contents

- THE SKIN -

MY STORY
We gain our identity from our history and life situation.
This is not who we truly are.   3

FROZEN
We each look different depending on our age but
we haven't always looked this way.   4

A MISERABLE DAY
Our interpretation of simply what is, can cause us misery.   6

PATIENCE
Practicing patience transforms how we look, how
we act and how we approach life's situations.   7

LISTENING WITH THE HEART
The way we listen to others makes all the difference.   9

PRESENCE BEATS INTERESTING
Being present and still have more long term
benefits than worldly temptations.   10

CHARITIES
The feigned friendliness of those asking for money
brings up a feeling of irritation.   11

THE EMOTIONAL RIDE
Our emotions can turn us into slaves if we don't
see them for what they are and take some control.   13

- THE BROWN BITS -

- THE FLESH -

- THE SEED -

Introduction

Life is mostly froth and bubble.
Two things stand like stone:
Kindness in another's trouble,
Courage in your own.

Ever since I was a child, short rhyming verses like this one by Adam Lindsay Gordon have given me an instant sense of delight. It only takes a few seconds to both read and digest such wonderful wisdom. I guess it should come as no surprise then that my first book is a collection of rhyming verses, just like this one. Thanks to mum, my childhood was filled with Dr. Seuss story books and it was the joy of the rhyming words that contributed to my desire to read the story to the end. Also, I loved the wisdom of his rhymes, such as this one:

You have brains in your head.
You have feet in your shoes.
You can steer yourself
Any direction you choose.

The Sioux Indians are credited with saying that,

The longest journey you will make in your life
is from your head to your heart.

Think of how you feel when you're in the flow with a project you're enjoying or mentally and physically relaxed in one of your favourite places. Perhaps you're taking in a painting that moves you or fully listening to the sound of a stream, a beautiful piece of music or the laughter of a child you hold dear. Remember the feeling you have with a book you just can't put down and wish would never end. I'll never forget how I felt when I arrived at the last page of Ken Follett's novel, *The Pillars of the Earth*. It was like saying goodbye to a close friend I just wasn't ready to farewell.

Like these beautiful moments in life, poetry too can help us on this journey from the head to the heart – our home of quiet stillness and peace.

For much of the time, most of us live in the head which is full of thoughts that come and go. We often allow these impermanent thoughts to pull us to the past or project us into the unknown future. They can bring up emotions like guilt, revenge, regret or worry. Although they only exist in our imagination, we allow the thoughts to take on some kind of permanency. Mindfulness can bring us back into the present moment and give us a gentle nudge to appreciate consciously, through our senses, each moment of this precious life, as it arises, moment by moment, breath by breath.

If we want to feel real, long lasting change, then mindful awareness needs to become part of our everyday life. I like to think of it as a daily joyful commitment to mindfulness practice which weaves itself into each moment I live. As Dr. Gordon Livingston reminds us in his wonderful book, *Too Soon Old, Too Late Smart*, "The tension between simplicity and effort works itself out in our daily lives. If we believe in the sudden transformation, the big score, we are less likely to pursue the harder and less immediately satisfying work of becoming the people we wish to be."

Life's a Mango is part of the mindfulness movement. It's a messenger that is contrary to the autopilot, busy, stressed out, reactive way of living. It's a move towards taking the time now to accept whatever is happening in a conscious way. It's a move towards surrendering to The Now, however it looks. It reminds us that we are each a human being with an inner awareness, a life force that connects us all and goes beyond our mere human labels like race, gender, nationality and belief systems.

When I was growing up, there was a daily reminder for me of taking time in life to smell the roses. There was an old framed sign on the wall of our rumpus room which read:

It's the roses in life
That make us feel great.
The ones on the grave,
Well, I think they're too late.

– Uncle Ben

Ever since I was a teenager, I've devoured religious, self-help, new-age, personal development, psychology and philosophy books. I've always underlined, highlighted and made notes in the margins – like a school or university student does in a textbook. What I'm doing is interacting with the words on the page so that they become a part of me. Like many of you, I've spent much of my life on the path of spiritual seeking. Now, when I go to a bookshelf at home, my favourite books are those that I can pluck off the shelf, open at any page and receive an instant gift of inspiration to guide me on my way. The words that I see help me to remember who I am and the direction I wish to go in. For me, it's the combination of wanting to use my gifts and to benefit others that makes life meaningful and motivates me to get out of bed in the morning.

Just like my favourite kinds of books, *Life's a Mango* is one that you can leave by your bedside or on your coffee table knowing that you are only a few uplifting verses away from feeling more inspired about life. It will help you to see things from a gentler perspective. Think of this book as a daily dose of sweet medicine
which will have you feeling just that bit kinder and more open-hearted as you interact with others during the day.

It was Albert Einstein who said,

There are only two ways to live your life.
One is as though nothing is a miracle.
The other is as though everything is a miracle.

Life's a Mango will remind you to live life according to the philosophy of his second option. There are so many books out there offering valuable lifestyle advice. How do we take that advice off the page and make it our own? We each find our own way of doing that. For me, it's by writing and reciting inspirational rhyming verse. I've taken some of the wisdom I've learnt over the years and woven it into everyday happenings so that you can see a mundane situation in a more magical, mindful way. Just like Dr Seuss, I reckon the message becomes easier to digest and remember if it's through rhyme.

As the second edition of *Life's a Mango* goes to print, life as we know it has changed. The global situation reminds us quite poignantly of the impermanence and unpredictability of life. The famous Polish physicist, Maria Salomea Skłodowska (Marie Curie), so wisely said,

Nothing in life is to be feared, it is only to be understood.
Now is the time to understand more, so that we may fear less.

Like so many of you, I have experienced sickness. When I was diagnosed with post-viral fatigue, I was bed ridden for many weeks. The symptoms were like that of chronic fatigue. I felt like a battery that was impossible to recharge. Strangely, I didn't fear it, fight it or resent it. Perhaps unconsciously I was saying, *Stop the world. I want to get off.* For some reason I accepted my condition and surrendered to what was happening.

As I lay in bed watching inspirational YouTube videos of Eckhart Tolle and His Holiness the Dalai Lama, I suddenly had the strong desire to transform what I was hearing into rhyming verse. I pulled out an old notebook and wrote down a poem. Then came another and then another. Every day my husband would come home from work and I would show him yet another poem. Fifty-four poems later and with the encouragement of family and friends, I was ready to self-publish the first edition of *Life's a Mango*.

It was William Shakespeare who said,

> *Sweet are the uses of adversity,*
> *Which, like the toad, ugly and venomous,*
> *Wears yet a precious jewel in his head.*

If it hadn't been for that post-viral fatigue, I would never have given myself the chance to stop and listen to my inner creative voice. My higher self was giving me an opportunity to express thoughts and emotions that had been laying dormant in my heart for years; some since childhood. What an incredible sense of relief it was to finally give those thoughts and feelings a voice and to see them in front of me on the paper. As the Buddhist teachings remind us, every single thing in life that is perceived as a difficulty can be transformed into something positive on the path to enlightenment. We are our own alchemists.

Undoubtedly, the best part about publishing a book is the feedback you receive from readers or listeners who tell you they have been moved by your work. Since the first edition, I've connected with many people of different ages and backgrounds and this connection has filled me with joy.

When people are moved and empowered by the words I have written, I feel a shared sense of intimacy and humanity. I'm reminded of the words from the movie, *Avatar* and the Zulu practice of Sawubona, *I see you.*

I love easy-to-understand, inspirational poetry that rhymes, and I hope you do too. With its mixture of mindfulness, wisdom and humour, it's my deepest hope that the verses I've written will assist in transforming your ordinary way of thinking into a way that is more extraordinary; one that is kinder, more appreciative and grateful. This attitude means that you and I, through our words and actions, can be more beneficial to ourselves and to all those we come into contact with.

We are each like a pebble on the surface of a pond.

Let's remember what the wise ones tell us: Everything that happens is an opportunity to transform our mind; to learn and to grow. When we accept and don't resist what is, the fear starts to diminish and we relax, open and connect.

As you travel along the road less travelled, let *Life's a Mango* be your trusted companion on the lifelong journey from the head to the heart.

The voyage of discovery is not in
seeking new landscapes but in
having new eyes.

Marcel Proust

The Skin

– hard to swallow

These poems deal with necessary life lessons that are hard for us to accept at times. Although they may lead us to a better place, it can feel like we are taking bitter medicine before we finally arrive at our destination.

My Story

This is my story.
This is who I am.
This is my name, and
My body is glam.

This is my country and
This is my race.
This is my gender and
This is my face.

This is my religion.
This is my house.
This is my car and
This is my spouse.

Take all these labels,
And throw them away.
It's the work of the ego
That's here at play.

Ego loves you to think
You **are** all of these things.
They just create problems,
Tie you up in your strings.

We identify with
Labels, but they're not true.
We feel they are though,
And they stick like glue.

Think of how sugar
Dresses up and looks sweet;
As a cake, as a candy,
As a jam donut treat.

They all look so fancy,
But look close and see;
It's just sugar dolled up
Looking pretty for me.

Look past the appearance,
And there you will see
We're all the same really -
Her, him, you and me.

Strive not to be a success, but rather to be of value.
– Albert Einstein

Frozen

We see people frozen;
Frozen in time.
Was once a young girl
Who knew how to climb.

As the voice becomes soft,
And the bones become weak.
The hair greys and thins,
Need a pad 'cause I leak.

White spots on the legs,
Dark marks on my hand,
Lines etched on my face,
Food starts to taste bland.

It really is weird
How the outside does change.
Look at me in a photo;
The shock is quite strange.

Your essence within
Still remains clear,
But the body and skin
To the mirror say fear.

It just makes you realise
That the way you relate
Depends on your age;
It bears so much weight.

Kids on the internet
Can pretend to be old.
Get people's respect
'Cause nobody's been told.

When I go to a shop
And I start to speak,
They're staring at fifty plus
Not at twenty, so sweet.

We need to see past
The face that is ageing.
All these moments of life,
Which have been engaging.

When I was a girl small,
Never dreamed for a mo'
That I would be old
Like my nana and so,

Now I have more respect
For the olds that I see.
I imagine the stories
And their past history.

So many movies
Play around with this theme.
People get old, yet
They still long to be seen.

jencompton.com

It's a number of days.
It's not really *old;*
A life time of moments,
A story that's told.

You will be amazed
By the things they can tell.
Their thoughts and their travels,
Tales from heaven to hell.

It's so easy to see people
As if frozen in time;
Like thinking a clock face
Has always shown nine.

So next time your brain
Says that face is *old,*
Find a better word.
Not frozen; it's gold.

Show your grandchild
A photo of you from the past.
What a shock they will get
To see *you,* that's a blast!

They can't quite believe
You could look so young.
Your face and your body,
Time: the damage it's done!

Perhaps the gift wrap
Looks worn on the outside,
Not the present within
Which is where *you* reside.

May you **be** healthy,
May you live long.
Take your B vitamins
So your mind remains strong.

Read Dr. Bredesen's
The End of Alzheimer's.
You won't lose your marbles.
Be healthy old timers.

If you keep your thoughts bright,
Grateful and kind,
Your outside may fade
But your essence – divine.

Age is an issue of mind over matter. If you don't mind, it doesn't matter.
– Mark Twain

A Miserable Day

Are you sure it's really
A miserable day?
The rain is falling, and
The sky is grey.

It's just the weather.
It's what you said;
Your thought of misery
Gets locked in your head.

When something happens,
The thoughts that you bring
Change the suchness of nature,
Distort everything.

We start to make stories
From stuff and we moan.
The stories take on
A life of their own.

The misery you feel
Is not from what happened.
It's the thoughts you impose
That make you feel rotten.

It is what it is,
She did what she did.
Let go of the story;
Accept what is lived.

It's the layers you add
To the suchness of life
That cause you trouble
And get you in strife.

Be calm and **be** still.
Let go of the thought.
It won't make things better.
You'll only get caught.

Forgive them their actions,
Realise it's true:
They are where they're at.
It is good for you.

Just know that things happen
And they always will.
Drop interpretation.
Be present and still.

There is nothing either good or bad, but thinking makes it so.
– William Shakespeare

jencompton.com

Patience

No way it's a weakness
This patience of yours.
Takes courage and practise,
Comes from a virtuous cause.

We all know that person
Who's patient and kind.
Doesn't come by accident;
They work on their mind.

When we're patient, we don't
Flinch when there's harm.
Mean words, kicks or punches
Are no cause for alarm.

A person who's patient
Knows that anger is bad.
Can cause much suffering,
Makes others feel sad.

That patient person has
A calm, gentle glow.
Their presence and grace
Help them go with the flow.

There's no attachment to good
Nor aversion to pain.
They accept what is and
Don't try to seek gain.

That person who's patient
Doesn't want to do harm.
Though you may be cruel,
Their behavior stays calm.

Wear patience like armour
As you go into battle.
When they push your buttons,
They're less likely to rattle.

Just know that this person
Is your negative karma.
Feel compassion for him.
Bad thoughts do not harbour.

The world is full of
Many people unkind.
You can't get rid of them
So best work on **your** mind.

Meditate each day
On the beauty of peace.
Less anger arises and
Patience will increase.

You'll feel calmer and softer
When with that angry dude.
He can't make you angry
'Cause your mind is subdued.

There'll always be hardships,
Disappointments and pain,
But if you lash out, get mean,
You've got nothing to gain.

Patience is a virtue.
Yes, that's what they say.
A cause for beauty in next life
And better relations today.

When you practice patience,
You'll see your best version too.
Less reactive, more present.
Others feel safe around you.

When they know they can say
What's just on their mind
Without you barking, reacting,
They'll see you as so kind.

Be patient with self.
Be patient with friends.
Be patient with life,
And so misery ends.

Patience is a key element of success.
– Bill Gates

Listening with the Heart

When someone is talking,
What do you do?
Does mind tend to wander
To other things too?

When someone is talking,
Interrupt with a word?
Stop their flow of thought
So you can be heard?

When someone is talking,
Your mind starts to create
What it will say next
When there is a break.

This is not listening;
It's reacting to words.
The person who's speaking
Is not truly heard.

To listen to someone,
Is to allow them to **be**.
You're there as a presence,
And that sets you free.

When you listen to someone,
Stay still and alert.
Listen with heart;
You're less likely to hurt.

Instead of thinking
What you will say now,
Keep yourself present.
Their thoughts you allow.

Don't try to be witty,
Clever or trite.
Just listen with heart and
You will get it right.

*The word listen **contains the same letters as the word** silent.*
– Alfred Brendel

Presence Beats Interesting

Awareness and presence
Can seem rather flat.
At least so says the ego
Who believes in all that.

The ego does *interesting*,
It does *future* and *past*
But this present moment?
Please, just don't ask!

Give me a theory,
An opinion or fact.
These are more interesting
Than present contact.

Presence is Aliveness,
It's Stillness and Now.
The ego can't stand that.
It will drag you somehow

To the TV, a smartphone,
A computer or magazine.
Anything really;
It needs to be seen.

Don't fall for its tricks,
It's cunning and sly.
Being present is worth
More than money can buy.

So you may ask,
Why is **now** just so special?
Why do I have to **be**
Present and settled?

Because IT is real,
It's truth, it is here.
Without living this moment,
You are caught up in fear.

The world IS interesting.
Yes, that is true.
But if you get trapped there,
You'll never **be** you.

Whatever you do,
Wherever you are,
Be aware of your presence
And then you'll go far.

Whatever interesting
Stuff's going on,
Feel the essence inside you.
Don't fall for the con.

Remember He said:
***Be** in this world but not of it.*
Wise words from a man
Who was a great prophet.

Be in the world but not of the world.
– John 15:19, Holy Bible

Charities

They come up to you
Smiling, looking their best.
For me, insincere,
OK. Here comes the test.

With bright, happy faces
They try to get money.
It has me annoyed.
I don't find it funny.

You know that their greeting
Is not from the heart.
They're saying hello so
From your money you'll part.

It's the same when they ring
To tell me their call
Is *just* to say thank you
For past giving to poor.

That's all very well,
But it just isn't true.
They're calling to get cash,
Not *just* to thank you.

When I give money
To those who are poor,
I get to choose when
They come to the door.

When it's the Salvos,
I'm normally fine.
They do good stuff;
Their giving – divine.

What makes me stew
Is the way some pretend
To like me so much;
As if I'm their best friend.

If you need to get money
Then stick to the point.
Please don't be over polite;
My feet you anoint.

When I give 'cause I want to
It just feels so good.
Not asked or ordered,
Is that understood?

If I see a good cause
I will give them money.
It's a choice I have made.
My heart feels so sunny.

We all have our triggers
And mine seem to be
Those ringing or asking
With voices chirpy.

Why does it make me
Inside feel so mad?
I need to **be** kinder
'Cause I could make them sad.

I already give
To many a good thing.
Don't want to be asked
When the phone it does ring.

How about when you give,
But it's just not enough.
They send you a letter
Asking you for more stuff!

Just made a donation
And you're feeling fine.
In comes the mail;
They want more; what a crime!

I guess the question is this –
Would I give at all
If I never did get
A knock or a call?

So many in need,
So many without,
But you can't give to all.
Of that, there's no doubt.

So next time they call,
How will I respond?
Breathe in and then out,
And pretend I am fond

Of the text they must read,
Of the job that they do.
They're just trying to help
Poor people, it's true.

I'll wait till they've finished.
I'll stay calm and still.
I'll try to **be** kind.
Please. Oh, yes, yes, I will.

For it is in giving that we receive.
– Saint Francis of Assisi

jencompton.com

The Emotional Ride

There are so many of them;
It's hard to keep count.
First a thought and then
Emotions' effects can mount.

Our senses take in the world;
Everything that's around, then
Pleasant/unpleasant/neutral –
Our mind chooses, it's found.

If we don't like that thing
Or that thought in our head,
Up comes an emotion,
And down its path we are lead.

We're sure it's the stuff from
Outside us that's the key.
Blame it on that person.
It couldn't be me!

Perhaps it's *Sadness*,
Rejection or *Doubt*.
Worry or *Fear*, your concerns
Are too many to count.

We're not even aware
That they're running the show.
Thoughts and emotions just lead.
Our body, words, actions follow.

We're caught in their grip
Like a dog with a chain.
There must be a way out
From this suffering and pain.

Well, there is my dear friends,
And with you I'll now share:
We observe them, stay **curious,**
But don't fall into their snare.

Emotions come up for a reason.
Look deep. Use them as info.
But separate trigger and meaning.
Then their purpose you'll know.

When there's something you don't like
Or a thought gets you going,
Be aware. Catch the feeling,
And you'll stay with more knowing.

Not caught in the story,
Instead address the root cause.
Stay with the feelings
As your heart opens doors.

When your buttons are pushed and
Your mind starts to twitch,
It signals a message that
You have a need to address.

Instead of entering
Inside the *Anger* bubble,
Stop and observe it before
It gets you into trouble.

Stay with it and breathe.
Remain **balanced** and wise.
Hello, Anger my friend.
I will not you despise.

I won't step in your bubble
Nor push you away.
I'll stay present and watch you
Pass through me. Pop! No dismay.

All sound too easy?
Well, yes, it takes skill,
But as we learn to observe them
We'll be happier still.

Less mountains of excitement
Or valleys of woe.
As we watch emotions
In our mind, come and go.

Don't stop them from knocking;
We still open the door,
But no yanking around now.
At their mercy no more.

There's now some control
As we see the emotions
That before caused us havoc,
Ill will and commotion.

You'll be pleased and delighted
How your life is more calm.
Less reactive, more balanced.
Your emotions don't harm.

Anger and Sadness,
Shame and Despair.
Neither follow nor shut out.
Just look. **Be aware.**

Give support to yourself
Like you would to a friend.
Be kind and **be** gentle.
A helping hand you can lend.

You'll feel lighter and younger,
Less stressed and uptight.
Your mind training helps you see
Their bark is bigger than bite.

Be aware and **be balanced**.
Be curious and just breathe.
Learn to live with emotions,
Live your life with more ease.

No one can make you feel inferior without your consent.
– Eleanor Roosevelt

Judging

When you see others
Do you tend to judge?
It can get in the way,
So here comes a nudge.

When the voice in the head
Starts to rant and to rave,
They're *nasty* or *ugly*,
They're *bossy* or *brave*.

Just stop for a minute
And bring yourself back.
You think this of others
But yourself you attack.

The more we judge others;
Label who we think they are,
More likely we judge us
For not reaching the bar.

Media makes us feel
Too this or too that.
Our body's not perfect;
Of course, we're too fat.

Expectations are huge
How we're supposed to look.
Can get you down some.
Compare models in book.

Have you noticed a cat?
You may think she's *ugly*.
But she has no label,
Even if she's pudgy.

The cat has no mirror.
It cannot compare
To all other cat forms.
If so, she would stare.

My fur is no good.
It's too coarse, it's too grey.
I can't go outdoors!
She'd meow with dismay.

If there were no mirrors
And no media too,
We'd accept who we are,
And I'd judge less of you.

What a beautiful world
I know it would be
If we loved each other.
I see you in me.

Love sees through the form.
Doesn't see *fat* or *thin*.
Just sees the spirit that
Lies there deep within.

jencompton.com

It sees past the outside,
Culture, skin kind.
Does not pigeon hole
For this makes us blind.

We accept it as norm;
Judgement lives in our head.
Constantly having thoughts,
By appearances fed.

Try not to judge.
Just accept what you see.
Tell the brain to be quiet,
And this sets you free.

I know it's not easy.
Believe me, it's not.
From every direction
The judgements run hot.

Your mind comes from one side,
The media another,
Then your sister or spouse.
Our joy, it can smother.

You're *beautiful* now.
That goes too for me.
No need to be different;
Rejoice and just **be**.

Give ourselves a hard time
And project on to other.
No one's living up.
Let's all run for cover!

Let's **be** like the cat.
No perception of *who*.
Pretend you can't see
This form I call *you*.

When I tend to give
Myself a hard time,
I start to feel lousy,
And this is a crime.

Constantly asking
How do I measure up?
A dangerous question.
How *cute* is a pup?

Give yourself a hard time,
You inflict yourself pain.
You can't **be** the light;
You've got nothing to gain.

I'm OK – You're OK
Is the name of a book.
When we look at life so
It runs smooth as a brook.

Be like the sun which
Shines forth on us all.
The *ugly* and *pretty*,
The *short* and the *tall*.

It doesn't use labels,
Choose who gets the light.
Its warmth and its life force;
We all have the right.

Others will judge you.
That's their ego inside.
Don't judge them back though
Or you'll both collide.

If we judge each other,
Race, looks, wealth and age.
We're always prejudiced,
Never on the same page.

We're all here for a while;
It's not very long.
Be kind to yourself.
Know we all belong.

You'll start to blossom.
Rejoice in the day.
I am that I am
Is your mantra to say.

If you judge people, you have no time to love them.
– Mother Teresa

Trust in Life

You get disappointed
By people and things.
You feel somehow let down.
Does this have a ring?

People will fail us;
They will let us down,
But when we accept that
There's no need to frown.

Trusting in people
Is like trusting in snow
To warm up your body
From your head to your toe.

The real trust comes by
Trusting in life.
Let it flow through you;
You will have less strife.

Surrender to The Now,
And **be** the whole space.
Let the contents evolve,
And it will bring grace.

As you have trust for
The moments that come,
You'll start to live by
The beat of its drum.

No coincidences
Or strange surprises.
All part of the plan
As this moment arises.

You appreciate more
The people you meet.
They've come for a reason;
You're in for a treat.

Just like the flowers
Put trust in the bees,
You put trust in life
And things flow with ease.

Don't resist or refuse
What comes up in the space;
Labelled *good* or *bad*,
You won't want to erase.

If someone hurts you,
There's a lesson to learn.
That person's just human;
There's no need to spurn.

Let's say you lose money,
And life looks real grim.
If you trust in life,
Like a fish you will swim.

On and on through water
You glide and you go,
With forms coming up
Like in some movie show.

You trust in your essence;
That feeling within.
Keeps you connected.
Know now you will win.

No matter what happens
In the movie you're in,
If you trust in The Now,
Miracles begin.

You'll take more interest
In what life throws up,
From the daily mundane,
To a newly born pup.

So decide here and **now**
To give up trusting people,
Or you may get hurt like
A falling church steeple.

When you see so clear
That people have fault,
You won't expect them to
Keep silent like a vault.

Once this expectation
Is out of the way,
You'll feel more relaxed
As you start to play.

The game of trust in
The game of life
Will improve the lot
Of husband and wife.

Don't try to control;
To get everything right.
This makes life rigid;
Always in fight or flight.

Say to yourself that
You trust in life's plan.
Be willing to play,
And know that you can.

All I have seen teaches me to trust the creator for all I have not seen.
– Ralph Waldo Emerson

jencompton.com

People and Things

Do you think that there's
Something that makes you whole?
A person? A trip?
A job? Show? A role?

We think that this thing
Will make us complete,
But when we wake up,
We're in for a treat!

It really is a
Bit like Halloween.
There's a scary presence
Beyond what is seen.

At first things seem great.
Everything is just swell.
But soon that good thing
Reminds you of Hell.

They say love is blind.
You'll see this is true.
The faults of your mate
Will start to come through.

Now, here's the test;
Just what you must do:
You use your mate's faults
So you can **be** new.

Each problem you have
Is a blessing you see.
If you look at it right,
You'll know that clearly.

Let's say your soul mate
Is one angry dude.
You get to show patience;
You can change the mood!

So often we see
The faults of another
More clearly than ours,
Which we tend to smother.

Now don't run away.
Don't moan or be blue.
Use the demons you feel
To transform, yes, YOU!

Things start to change
When you look at them right,
From boring to great,
From dull to so bright.

So next time your mate
Gives you a hard time,
Step away from yourself,
And try to **be** kind.

They are not perfect.
They too have their pain.
Use it, just use it.
Go beyond the mundane.

Don't get caught in the trap
Of reaction and fight.
See it as a blessing.
You'll be alright.

For nothing is what
It appears to be.
The judgement, the hurt
Is your destiny.

It's opportunity.
Yes, that is the find.
What bugs you the most
Is a gift from Divine.

If you change the way you look at things, the things you look at change.
– Wayne Dyer

The Voice in the Head

Can you hear it?
A voice that talks in your head.
It chatters away.
It likes to be fed.

Negative thoughts are what
It really likes best.
On and on they can go
Without any rest.

Next time that you hear it,
Stop a minute and say,
*Oh, that's you again but
I choose not to play.*

Out of your head and
Go into your chest.
Sense yourself breathing
Where you know it feels best.

Bring your mind to your body,
Feel your hands and your feet,
Your shoulders, your elbows,
Now that's it, you're sweet.

Next time that the voice says,
Hey, Listen to me!
Say, *Not right now thanks.*
You'll set yourself free.

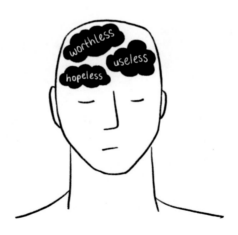

What we think, we become.
– Shakyamuni Buddha

Seeking

Are you seeking something
That you haven't got?
A new car? A new house?
A perfect holiday spot?

Perhaps you're a seeker;
You want to be Buddha.
That's a worthy pursuit;
No would-a or should-a.

Stop searching for things that
You don't right now hold.
Be content and **be** present
'Cause this feels good as gold.

Are you seeking a person?
Or seeking a thing?
To be something different?
Just what will it bring?

Material or not,
If you are a seeker
You're not quite content.
It could make you weaker.

It may make you grumpy
'Cause you're never there.
That place in the future
You believe to be rare.

You try and do practice;
Do all the right stuff,
But if you're not present
You'll just huff and you'll puff.

Seek if you must now;
Enlightenment calling,
But stay in the moment.
There's no way it's stalling.

You can **be** a seeker
And **be** open to **now**.
Don't devalue this moment.
On and on you do plough.

A tree doesn't say,
I don't like who I am.
It accepts and is present;
All part of the grand plan.

jencompton.com

When you constantly want
That thing in the future,
You're mostly frustrated;
In a real stupor.

Be grateful for **now**.
Let go of the search.
Like a bird or a tree,
You are your own church.

When we seek, we're not here.
Always travelling To.
Feel your awareness, and
Be content to **be** you.

To **be** who you are,
You do not need time.
No stepping stone to next;
Forget future. You're fine.

Your aliveness will grow,
You'll **be** like a flower.
When you're happy with **now**,
You are the power.

*It is through gratitude for the present moment that
the spiritual dimension of life opens up.*
– Eckhart Tolle

A Different Life

We can't get a park,
Or our restaurant is closed.
The wine's not as good,
Or the bread's a day old.

We need to travel
To faraway lands
To see for ourselves
How others can't plan:

You wake up in the morn.
Not sure where you'll go.
Like a leaf in the breeze;
Get tossed to and fro.

Perhaps there's a spot
Where you can find food.
You're always hungry;
It affects your mood.

There's a man who is kind
With a stall that makes tea.
If you help serving chai,
He'll pay you a small fee.

Oh my gosh! What delight!
Your heart takes a leap.
These few silver coins
Get to buy you a small treat.

Like a dog with a prize,
You protect it from harm.
Sit under a bridge and
Pull it out, feeling calm.

This moment is sacred.
Who knows when you'll next eat?
You take your first bite, and
Savour warm, juicy heat.

You want to devour it,
To gobble it down,
But you eat with reverence.
There's hardly a sound.

Once it is over, you
Could eat so much more,
But the stomach is grateful;
Feels rich and not poor.

You're safe and alive
Alone under the bridge.
With food in your stomach.
Now. All that there is.

It soon will be nightfall.
You need to find a safe place.
Men go looking for kids
To sell, use, deface.

This is how some kids
Live out their daily life.
In lands far away;
Real trouble and strife.

Since they own nothing
They see with different eyes;
Live like animals
Beneath the night skies.

There's a movie called
Lion about a boy lost.
Great kindness, compassion;
No matter the cost.

Do not feel guilty
You earn a month's pay.
Use it to help others;
Make the most of this day.

Step outside your bubble.
Your heart then expands
To brothers and sisters
In faraway lands.

There are people in the world so hungry, that God
cannot appear to them except in the form of bread.
– Mahatma Gandhi

When Things Start to Pile Up

The list seems so long,
There is so much to do.
Just the thought of it all!
Where to start? Not a clue.

So often the dread
Is just in the thoughts.
They take us on journeys
And get us all caught.

Be calm and **be** still.
Be present and breathe.
When your mind is relaxed,
You'll feel much more at ease.

Look at the list,
And make a good start.
Be present and joyful.
Hey, don't fall apart.

Don't resist what is there;
Just do it in steps.
Keep your mind on the job,
You'll make good progress.

Stay in the present.
Stay in The Now.
Do what you can.
On and on you do plough.

Just keep going with
Joy and you will see,
Very soon you'll be done,
Your heart full of glee.

I hear and I forget. I see and I remember. I do and I understand.
– Confucius

The Languages of Love

Each of us has a
Different way to show love.
When you figure this out
You'll swap raven for dove.

The first one is **service** –
Doing washing or chores.
May be your number one,
But to your partner, it bores.

For you though, it's great
When others help you out.
This must be your love language
If you are in doubt.

The second is **touch** –
A caress or a hug.
Some love to receive them,
But for others, you'll bug.

You may long to touch,
To show how you feel,
But your loved one might flinch
And act cold as steel.

The third is **language** –
The words that we hear.
I love you. You're great.
Are important; endear.

Some get embarrassed
By these words that you utter.
But you long to hear them –
It makes your heart flutter.

Spending quality time –
Is what comes up next.
Two souls together,
Not sending a text.

It may be a board game
Or camping outdoors.
A walk hand-in-hand,
Or going out to the stores.

This may not be one
That you label divine.
You're just content to see them
From six pm through to nine.

The last one is **presents** –
Material stuff.
Buying gifts to please them
May get you off the cuff.

Some long for gifts
Whilst others don't care.
You thought they'd be pleased,
But their weak smile brings despair.

We all have a love language
That we think's more important.
If it's not the same as your partner's,
You may feel a bit daunted.

I'm happy to say that
Our second is **quality time.**
Spending moments together,
And we are mostly fine.

Try to think now of which
Love language to use
To make your loved one happy.
So, you get to choose.

Will you iron their clothes?
Or give them a big hug?
Tell them you love them?
Wine and cheese on a rug?

Buy them something nice
You know they'll adore?
Which one of these languages
Speaks to their core?

Pick the right one now
Which will have an impact.
Think carefully so
Their love you'll attract.

If you're showing your love
With the way *you* like best,
The relationship suffers.
It may lack some zest.

Now, how does your loved one
Like love to be shown?
Think this quite often and
They're less likely to moan.

You may love to hear words,
But perhaps they like *service*
So don't tell them they're great
'Cause it just makes them nervous.

Instead, make their bed
Or fix something that's broken.
Cook them a nice meal,
Do an act, a small token.

Your relationship will flower.
They'll appreciate you more,
And when they look in your eyes
They'll love you to your core.

To the world you may be one person, but to one person you are the world.
— Bill Wilson

Antidotes for Anxiety

You can feel it coming,
Just the thought fills you with dread.
Not another panic attack.
Please no! You reach for your med.

Your heart starts to beat faster,
Your mind's full of *What if?*s
Your breathing is shallow.
Won't be right till it shifts.

When anxiety strikes:
Lock your hands behind head.
Lean back and breathe in deep.
You're here **now** with less dread.

Your breathing will slow and
You'll **be** more in The Now.
Less catastrophic thoughts
As you say out loud:

My eyes can see this.
My hands touch the skin.
My ears hear the birds.
I'm here and I'll win.

I give thanks for this life,
For this moment, this day.
I'm here in the present.
Yes, this vow I do say.

I just don't need to know
Everything happening on this earth.
Twitter, Facebook, the news;
At times, give them a wide berth.

I have daily rituals
Like starting with app *Calm*.
I scan my whole body:
Top of head, face, then down arm.

The panic may come, but
There's less fear from now on.
I am not the victim, but
The observer of sit-com.

My head talk is vital, but
It must not run the show.
I'm not its slave now, and
I'm more powerful than I know.

Relentless boss in the head
Is always putting me down.
Loves negative speech that
Seems like I might drown.

The boss is not me.
It does not run the show.
I stay present and breathe.
I trust and go with the flow.

We're constantly thinking,
But it can cause us such pain.
It can trigger an emotion.
Oh no, here we go again!

Learn to calm down
The winds of your mind.
You'll have more inner peace.
Yes, this you will find.

Come down from the head,
And **be** aware of your breath.
In for 4, hold for 7, breathe
Out for 8 counts, now rest.

Another great way is to
Lay on your bed with legs bent.
Stretch your arms behind you.
Feels like heaven's been sent.

Eat a good diet and
Please, get enough sleep.
Less sugar, drink and caffeine.
You're less likely to weep.

All of these tips rescue
Us from the thinking mind
That wants to control us
And have us living blind.

Have you heard of Bev Aisbett?
She helps you overcome panic.
Supports with managing anxiety.
You'll be calmer, less manic.

Another read that is helpful
Is *The Book of Hope*.
Has antidotes for anxiety
That will help keep you afloat.

Just believe you'll overcome this.
Be strong and stay true.
There are so many of us with it.
But together we'll get through.

Remember these tips, and
Give yourself a kind cuddle
As you navigate these waters
In your protective, white bubble.

Smile, breathe and go slowly.
– Thich Nhat Hanh

The Brown Bits

- that add character

These poems teach us that imperfections can actually be more beautiful than things that appear to be flawless. Without these character building moments and experiences, we wouldn't learn wisdom and resilience.

Pay It Forward

You order a coffee
And a croissant,
But as you go to pay
You tell them your want.

You'd like to pay more
To cover the cost of
The next person's coffee.
Now, you've gained and not lost.

Giving like this is
A beautiful act.
Try to do it sometimes,
And make it your pact.

Think of all the ways
That you can give more
To family and friends,
To strangers, the poor.

Hold a door open,
Let that car get in front,
Give someone some food.
Don't fish and don't hunt.

By giving like this
You forget yourself.
Less selfish thoughts now,
And you have more wealth.

When someone is kind
With a gesture or word,
You can pay it forward;
It's not so absurd.

I once paid the toll
For the car behind me.
It was rewarding,
And I felt so free.

Random acts of kindness
Make daily life magic.
Connect us to others
Like a big woven fabric.

You may send an email
To compliment or praise.
When it's done from the heart,
Their spirits you'll raise.

It really is cool
To live life this way.
There's a chance to practise
Right here. Now. Today.

Your acts, your money,
Your patience, your time.
Make somebody's day
By giving. Divine.

There's a book out there.
It's called *I like Giving*.
Will help you on your quest;
A New Way of Living.

Ask, *What can I give?*
Not, *What can I take?*
Your days will be fuller,
And magic you'll make.

How can I help?
Is the thought in your head
As you live out your life
Knowing you will be led:

To give and give more
To all those you meet.
These acts of kindness
Will make your life sweet.

It's not how much we give but how much love we put into giving.
– Mother Teresa

The Catch Up

As I drive to the café my
Thoughts jump ahead one hour;
What I'll say, how I'll act
As I engage with this power.

The filter in the mind is
Always right there in place.
What I hide, what I don't.
Will it save me from grace?

With some, I'm the listener.
With others, I talk more.
The ones I like best are
Where we both share the floor.

I know those who prefer
To talk about self
So I sit, listen well and
Ask them about health.

Then there's my mum
Who loves to listen with joy.
Hangs on each word I say,
Come on, don't be coy.

Others ask me questions,
But they're being polite.
If I talk more than a minute,
Their eyes drift to the right.

With some I'm on guard,
Scared to open too much.
Might be used as a weapon
So I stay light, *such 'n such.*

With some friends it feels like
A warm bubble bath.
You relax, you connect,
You talk and you laugh.

The time passes quickly,
And you're sad when it ends.
You love being with them,
These beautiful friends.

What I love most,
And I bet you do too
Is when you say something,
And friends ask for a review.

They're seeking more info,
Not just being polite.
They're trying to get you,
So they understand right.

My eyes just light up when
I know someone's listened.
Oh my gosh, we've connected.
My eyes start to glisten.

It feels like we're playing
A great game of ping-pong.
We hit the ball to each other,
And our rally is long.

As I take a keen interest
In the world of my friend,
She relaxes, opens up.
A kind message I send.

I give such a gift
When I let her just speak.
Forget myself for a while
And become a bit meek.

When the meeting is over
And she goes on her way,
She'll remember my gift
'Cause I let her have her say.

I didn't compete
Or take over the show.
I was gracious and kind.
In their heart, they just know.

You try not to judge them,
Or talk too much about you.
You just take delight
In their point of view.

It reminds me of my mum,
Who delights in my words.
With a friend, I give space
'Cause it's what she deserves.

My gift to her now
Is to see behind speech.
Work out her needs
As their meaning, they reach.

It feels like a therapist
Trying to get to the core.
Behind the words in her mouth,
Well, there's always much more.

As they realise it matters
To you, the words that they say,
They'll like and respect you.
Gosh! You might make their day.

So next time you catch up
With that friend that you know,
Stay curious and just listen.
See how they start to glow.

It's funny how friends
Can do this to me.
Wonder who I'll **be** today
When I meet them at 3?

A friend is someone who knows all about you and still loves you.
– Elbert Hubbard

The Look on Your Face

Be aware of the look
That you have on your face,
As you're walking around
From each place to place.

The look that you have
When your face is relaxed,
Can be nice to look at
Or it can look quite taxed.

Why does this matter?
I now hear you say.
Because it's a signpost
That you must display.

The people who pass you
Judge you by your face.
Not beauty or ugly;
What comes through is grace.

The thoughts that you have,
Whether they're mean or kind,
Start to show on your face,
And there you will find

That if you're anxious,
Nasty or down,
Your face will reflect this
With a scowl or a frown.

So try to stay present
With a smile on your lips.
Keep your eyes soft and focused.
Feel the grace that emits.

When others observe your
Look that is soft,
They naturally like you.
They'll tend not to scoff.

Have thoughts that are
Pleasant, peaceful and kind.
Put a smile on your face,
And then you will find

That others will treat you
With love and respect,
'Cause the sign you display says,
I'm here to connect.

Let the beauty of what you love be what you do.
– Rumi

Complaining

Sometimes we don't realise
How lucky we are.
We moan and we groan.
It won't get us far.

We get stuck in a rut
And everything's bad.
If we keep complaining,
It makes you and me sad.

Next time you're tempted
To say it's no good,
Using *no* and *not*,
And *wrong* and *should*,

Pull yourself up and
Say, *Hey! Wait a mo!*
I've got much to **be**
Grateful for and so,

Be grateful for food,
For your house and your clothes,
Your life, your family,
Your hands and your nose.

Pick up an orange,
And think of the sun
That shone on the fruit
Until it was done.

There are so many ways
We can say, *Thank you now.*
Just stop and **be** grateful,
And make it your vow.

Every time you get
Tempted to complain,
Say, *No! I don't want
To do that again.*

Thank you, I'm grateful.
Thank you so much,
For this day, for this life,
For this moment as such.

A Long Time Together

You have lived with another
For sixty whole years -
Through joys and through sorrows,
There've been laughter and tears.

As you stand at the altar
Feeling young, full of glee,
You have no idea
Of what you'll both see.

Their joy is ours and
So is their pain.
The successes and triumphs,
The losses and gains.

We learn words that can heal
And words that will wound.
Their habits, dislikes,
Which is their favourite spoon.

We get used to our spouse
Like a comfy old coat,
The two become one;
You're the white, s/he's the yolk.

The love that you felt
All those long years ago
Is nothing compared
To what you now know.

You've been a devil, a saint
And everything inbetween;
Considerate and helpful,
Annoying and mean.

Your partner has seen
It all, yes, siree!
But they're still by your side.
Amazed? You should be.

You were taken to places
You did not want to go,
But it's character building
And we reap what we sow.

Despite your differences,
You've stayed a strong team.
You've trusted one another,
On each other, you lean.

There are secrets you've shared
That must not be heard.
You've made an agreement,
And *Mum* is the word.

There've been so many tests
Of your love over time;
Too many to count.
You've been mean and then kind.

It's not easy to stay
With a person for life.
They get on your nerves, right?
Whether husband or wife.

You've travelled a lot
And shared beautiful moments.
Your love of nature;
Important component.

Cereal and toast,
Steak and red wine,
Seafood and salad,
Together you've dined.

Tea and coffee
Whiskey and beer,
White wine and red,
After 5, is it dear?

There's a big part of you
That others just don't see.
Reserved for your partner;
It's your special *me*.

There are less years ahead now
Than those that you've shared.
You look back on a journey,
And see how you've fared.

Two generous hearts
Feel just good as gold
As they see kids and grandkids
Whom they all helped to mould.

You've both been so giving
And supported us all –
Helped pick us up, dust us off
When we sometimes did fall.

We may not always
See eye to eye but
That's not important 'cause
There's love, won't deny.

With pride and with joy
On a job that's well done,
You are not so worried
When death, it may come.

You don't look as fresh
As you did in '58,
But you've stuck with each other,
And you've been a true mate.

You've counted your blessings
On this path you have travelled.
You've cared for each other
As life, it unravelled.

You both feel so grateful
That the other's still there
Through your worst and best versions,
Through times ugly and fair.

It's sure not a sprint
But a marathon with rests.
Just when the path's clear,
Life throws you some more tests.

You've been lover and friend,
Sometimes alley or foe.
You've comforted, cajoled,
Or been part of their woe.

Some pain you have kept
Locked away in your heart.
Not burdened your loved ones.
Such kindness, so smart.

Every emotion there is
Out under the sun:
You've been there, done that.
None left? Yes, there's one.

The one that is left
Is the final goodbye.
You know that it's coming.
Some fear of when you will die.

There may be a 70th
But then maybe not.
It just doesn't matter when
You give it all that you've got.

The love that you knew
Looks so different today.
At times you may not *feel* love,
But you've both come a long way.

Your partner's your retreat;
They're the way that you grow
To acceptance and patience -
Nothing you both don't know.

So, hats off to you two
For the journey you took.
Your God will be pleased
With your long marriage book.

If I know what love is, it is because of you.
– Hermann Hesse

Busy

How's your day been? Busy?
They often do say
When I'm at the checkout,
All ready to pay.

I yearn to reach them,
To state the facts.
I say, *No, not busy.*
Just quiet, relaxed.

They sometimes look shocked,
Oh, how could it be?
This person's not busy?
She must be lazy!

Be careful you don't
Live life like a hamster
With thoughts *I can't stop!*
This is not the answer.

It seems contrary, but
I've actually heard
Busy is like Lazy.
Yes, that seems absurd!

'Cause Busy takes you away
From your essence within.
It keeps you distracted,
And that is a sin.

When you keep busy,
You don't see what's in town.
The list in your head
May cause you to drown.

When you're constantly busy,
The present's not sacred;
Just a means to an end,
It makes you feel wasted.

So, what can I do?
I now hear you say.
My life is so busy.
I can't change it today.

Take time every day
To just go within.
Some moments in the morning,
And again in the evening.

Just feel your body;
Your essence within,
Your feet and your legs,
Your trunk and your chin.

Your day may be busy
Packed full to the brim, but
You'll have more awareness
Going out on a limb.

Beware of Busy
For it takes you away
From your true inner essence,
Which wants you to stay.

In the present, right here,
Right now where you're at.
You need to be focused.
You don't need flat chat.

Give respect to each moment
Now it has come.
It's sacred, it's beauty.
It's something you've won.

Busy will keep you
Focused on next.
Come back to The Now and
You won't be perplexed.

Nature does not hurry, yet everything is accomplished.
– Lao Tzu

Success

S is for the sight
To see journey ahead.
A vision of future
And by present be led.

U is for unlocking
Your potential within.
Open your heart, and
Let the journey begin.

C is for cherishing
This very moment.
Invite the now in;
Important component.

C is for consciousness;
Let it work through you.
Be the space for the art;
Your light will shine through.

E is for ego.
Of this, just let go.
Pretends to be best friend,
But is actually a foe.

S is for surrender
To the greater good.
Don't resist or push.
Accept. Understood?

S is for savour
All people and things.
In your life for a reason;
The wind under your wings.

This is real success, and
It's not found in money.
Have courage to dream, and
Life will be sunny.

It's not what you have,
How much silver or gold.
Be true to yourself,
Let success then unfold.

There may be fear
Of releasing the known.
Just trust and have faith;
Know you're never alone.

These words, they are true.
To your heart you must listen.
The best teacher for life,
Know you're on a mission.

Be bold and stay true.
Let this moment unfold.
Do what you love;
See life's good as gold.

Success is not a destination, but the road that you're on.
– Marion Wayans

Adults

Just 'cause they're older
Doesn't mean they know best.
If adults don't train the mind,
They can be a real pest.

Some use their years to
Bully and act mean.
You might still be a kid,
But you know what you've seen.

Some hit and some shout,
Speak rude and belittle.
They think they're the boss,
But their mind, it is brittle.

You're in a small body
So it's hard to get seen,
But your sensible words
May be wise, clear and clean.

Work on your mind, child.
Train it as you grow.
You'll **be** clam and alert,
More in tune now, you know?

You'll rise above the adults'
Anger and stress.
Their attitude to life:
Oh my, what a mess.

Send them thoughts of love,
Of gratitude, too.
Many sacrifices
They have made just for you.

As you train your mind,
You will feel a shift.
As you start to soften,
There's less of a rift.

Our parents and teachers
Can show us a lot.
Some are good models,
But some sure are not.

When people say things:
Sarcastic and rude,
Just sounds to the ears.
There's no need to feud.

Always say to yourself,
Not how I want to be.
Reject that model, and
You'll start to feel free.

The people I've known
Have all taught me stuff.
These poems I write
From moments. Some tough.

Step out of your skin, child.
Look down from a view.
All the people and places
Help to shape future YOU.

You can't see it yet,
But I'm fifty-four.
Every person, event:
Now I see what for.

Kindness comes dressed
In all different ways.
Doesn't always look nice,
But can guide you. It sways.

If you live with someone
Who you just don't like.
Treat them with kindness.
They're less likely to bite.

Their anger and rudeness
Hide much deeper things.
Show compassion and help.
Now, see what that brings.

As they shout or are mean,
Be still like a tree.
Pray for them too, *May you*
Free from suffering be.

If they are like fire, child
Then like water you are.
Their flames become smaller,
Less harm, they'll not scar.

See people around you
As jewels to collect.
Everyone can teach you.
Okay? Please don't forget.

The most potent muse of all is our own inner child.
– Stephen Nachmanovitch

A Problem

When you have a problem,
What's the best thing to do?
Should you think and think
And think it all through?

Analyse from here?
Analyse from there?
Going over it more
Until you despair?

Not the best method
To fix your concern.
You won't solve it this way.
You'll make yourself stern.

The solution you'll find
Is letting it **be**.
Be still and **be** present.
You'll set yourself free.

Drop down to the body,
To the breath in your chest.
Breathe in and out slowly.
You are now at rest.

When you can just **be**,
The solution will come
With calm clarity;
The answer you've won.

Thinking is form.
Our mind just pulsates
Away from the peace
Where the answer awaits.

Don't force the answer.
Have faith it will come.
Be with your essence,
And drop the re-run.

As you relax,
Still, calm and free,
The answer pops up;
As clear as can be.

The next time a problem
Has you in its grip,
Don't try to solve it
Till you have a fit.

Be calm, **be** alert,
Be patient and wise.
The answer will come like
First light at sunrise.

No problem can be solved from the same level of consciousness that created it.
– Albert Einstein

jencompton.com

Compassion

This word comes from empathy;
You want to ease another's pain.
You see them as you;
This view has much to gain.

It is consistent –
There are no ups and downs.
They may treat you bad, but
Your compassion resounds.

All beings: my mothers
In past lives have been.
They have been kind so I
Must repay them. I'm keen.

Those who meditate long
Have minds of wellbeing.
They wish to help others,
Eyes of love, all seeing.

Acts of compassion
Can change someone's life.
Your act of kindness
Cuts through like a knife.

Your heart starts to open.
You feel lighter and free.
You're the pebble in the pond;
Your way affects me.

No matter what happens,
Whether it's *good* or *bad,*
Your mind remains stable,
Neither *happy* nor *sad.*

If you just think of you,
Your misery will grow.
But cherish your sisters and
Your face, it will glow.

When you're wrapped in yourself,
You're more selfish and mean.
Caught up in your own bubble.
Others do not get seen.

Today, just decide
That you'll do one kind act.
No one may notice, but
Your mind changes. That's fact.

We have this wrong view
That our body is best.
This is not correct, and
You'll be put to the test.

Our ego pretends
To be friend but it's not.
See others as precious,
Your heart loses the knot.

Go read the Dharma.
Goggle FPMT.
Listen to lamas.
Your heart is set free.

I'm never quite sure
How I affect you.
When I have compassion,
My heart feels like new.

The Lost Art of Compassion
Is a beautiful read.
Makes your heart open,
It will plant the seed.

Do you see people's plight?
Are you aware of their needs?
See hunger, poverty?
Your mind will be freed.

When you bear the pain
Of sister or brother,
The joy that you have
Will selfish thoughts smother.

You're not yet bodhisattva,
But you're well on your way.
Take time to practice,
Do a bit every day.

Forgive and see others
As suffering too.
They're doing their best,
And they're just like you.

Compassion for self,
Compassion for others.
We're all in the same boat;
You, me, our mothers.

Instead of putting others in their place, put yourself in their place.
– Amish Proverb

Who Am I ?

I look in the mirror
And what do I see?
A person? A face?
But then, is that ME?

I have eyes of some colour,
A nose of some size,
Hair of some shade
And a skin tone besides.

The body I see
Is not really *mine*.
It's changing each moment,
And that is just fine.

Don't fall in love with
The image you see.
That's the ego which
Says, *Hey, look at me!*

It wants you to think that
You're more than the rest.
Your eyes and your body
Are definitely best.

Helps you go here and there
And do this and that,
But your body's not you,
And that is a fact.

So, who am I then
If the body I'm not?
You're who can feel it
When you stand in a spot.

Behind the eyes that can see,
The ears that can hear
Is an essence that's YOU
Which is always near.

So the next time you look
In the mirror and say,
Hey, gorgeous person,
I love you today!

Remember that everyone
Else feels the same.
They think that their body's
The top domain.

Believing that *you*
Are more special than *me*,
Causes some problems
As I'm sure you will see.

You're not your body.
Believe me, it's true.
You're the stillness, the essence
That lies within you.

Ageless body, Timeless mind.
– Deepak Chopra

Appreciation

There once was a woman
Who served her man hay.
He didn't like that at all.
He looked up in dismay.

What are you doing?
And *Where is my meal?*
He moaned and he shouted.
I'm sure you get the deal.

His wife stared at the plate,
And then said with focus
That by serving him hay,
She was sure he would notice.

He looked at her weird,
Not getting the picture.
She had to spell it out
Like reading a scripture.

These past 20 years,
I've put food on the table.
Cooked all your meals,
The best I was able.

Not once have you said
Well, thank you my dear.
This meal was delicious.
It went well with my beer.

I drove and I shopped,
I packed and I cooked
So you could have food.
For granted, me, you took.

So, how about your life?
Do you let loved ones know
You appreciate them
From their head to their toe?

We can become blind
To the people we love.
Need to see them afresh
Like some pure, white dove.

A squeeze or a smile,
A look or *thank you*
Is all that you need
To say or to do.

Just that small act
A difference can make,
If it's done sincerely.
Make sure it's not fake.

Nourishment for the soul
Is better than food.
It can lift our spirits,
Thank you changes the mood.

Just let them know that
You see beyond role,
Of wife or of husband.
Look through to the soul.

This little thing can
Transform your whole life.
From mundane and sad,
It cuts through like a knife.

Appreciation
Is being aware
Of those who you live with,
For beings who care.

Stop for a minute
And ask yourself how
You will show gratitude.
Come on, do it **now.**

Each day see loved ones
As a real precious gift.
Tell them or show them 'cause
Their spirits you'll lift.

It's not what I have in my life but who I have in my life that counts.
– J.M. Laurence

The Car Crash

This morning had a car crash
But I am OK. Thanks
To the kindness of others,
I'm still here today.

As I stood shaky and dazed
With my car all a wreck,
An angel called Margaret
Took control with respect.

She cared for us drivers,
Called police, ambos too.
Made sure we were alright;
No more could she do.

Then came Brian, the stranger,
And a neighbour with stools,
Luke and Claudia, the ambos,
Obeyed all of the rules.

Tow truck drivers were great,
And gave us good advice.
Helped us with paperwork and
They all were so nice.

Robert and Alison,
Rashnan and Craig,
All the staff at the hospital,
I have nothing but praise.

Karma is karma.
Be present **now**.
No matter what happens,
Make this your vow.

S**T sometimes happens,
But accept and **be** here.
There's always a lesson.
Have trust and not fear.

Courage is knowing what not to fear.
– Plato

Therapists and Parents

Don't listen to them.
They tell you your pain
Is 'cause of your parents.
You've got nothing to gain.

You'll spend lots of money
And talk yourself hoarse.
Drag you back to the past;
It's their fault, of course!

They want you to think
Parents are the villain.
Your issues and stuff,
Blame them a trillion.

It's an easy trap
If you're not careful.
You turned out this way
Because they were dreadful.

Now let's have a look
From a different view.
They did what they could
Mainly thinking of you.

They just did the best
With where they were at.
They weren't perfect beings,
Only humans at that.

Think of the good things.
Don't dwell on the bad.
Rejoice in the beauty.
If not, you'll get mad.

If you have emotions
Of anger, deceit,
These helped to mould you,
Get you on your feet.

When you are a parent
You'll see so too.
Not all goes to plan;
There are days when you spew.

The ego just loves
Your negative thought;
To dwell and to judge,
Like a lawyer in court.

You go over things
A thousand and one times,
Imagining alternatives;
A future divine.

This is like a river
Mourning its route,
A tree in autumn has
Some wish for green shoot.

The past is just that.
Let go of it **now**.
Release it, come on,
Do not to it bow.

Whatever they did,
Forgive them I say.
Just love them whoever
They are now today.

You may be scoffing
Or rolling your eyes,
But your throwing karma
Does not tell lies.

You won't have them long.
Rejoice in this hour.
Give them your love,
Don't let your mind sour.

Keep your heart open,
No matter the hurt.
This will take you further
Than dragging up dirt.

There are things they could
Have done, yes it's true,
But thinking of that
Is not healthy for you.

Look where you are.
Get up off the ground.
Feel the power of **now**,
And there is no bound.

Your parents are all
Part of the plan.
Take hold of the present.
Feel like Superman!

We never know the love of a parent till we become parents ourselves.
– Henry Ward Beecher

Your Role

Ever known someone
A very long time, but
They don't really know you?
They think that's just fine.

You feel like you're walking
Through a field full of mines.
You know what not to say,
Where not to cross lines.

You just don't feel safe.
You're always on edge.
Make one wrong move and
They'll push you off the ledge.

All your attention
Is on playing it safe.
You can't really relax;
You're not given the space.

Frightened of anger,
Of mean words, reject.
You try to get through it;
Not make them upset.

Because of this fear the
Relationship can't grow.
It's completely frozen.
There's nowhere to go.

They just can't see it.
You're playing a role.
Like puppet in a theatre,
The script covers your soul.

Beware of relaxing
With wine or with beer.
You'll let your guard down.
Your heart they will spear.

You kick yourself twice
For dropping your guard.
What you said upset them;
You dealt the wrong card.

You now have a choice:
Return to your role
Or once and for all
Say, *No* and **be** bold.

You know what is coming.
Feels like World War III.
They'll finally see you.
You'll set yourself free.

Sometimes the fear is
More than the wish
To **be** who you are.
There's fear of the shift.

jencompton.com

The anger, the shouting,
The threats, their attack,
Has you frozen in fear.
You just can't fight back.

So you have a choice
Which direction you'll take.
Keep playing the role
And feel like a fake.

If this sounds like you
Go inwards and ask,
Can I live like this?
Am I living a farce?

It won't feel easy to
Step out of the role,
But your spirit will soar;
Reveal now your soul.

Either there'll be a shift
Or you will move on.
Listen to your heart.
Now, sing your own song.

Nothing ever goes away until it teaches us what we need to know.
– Pema Chödrön

Airports

I'm at San Fran Airport
On my way to Spokane.
Feeling jet lagged but calm
As my mind tries not to plan.

Everyone's in transition
With at least one bag in tow.
Or now eating and drinking
With no place to go.

We're all here together
Yet united we're not.
We're like moving particles
As we drift from each spot.

Funny places these airports,
And they always remind me
That although on a journey,
It's wise to just **be**.

Everyone's either walking
From Arrivals to Gate Three,
Staring at airline screens
Or watching TV.

Now with smartphones,
Nobody is bored.
We're all plugged into devices.
Internet's the new Lord.

All the staff wear a lanyard
With their photo ID.
They try to make our transition
As pleasant as can be.

And then there's the posh shops
Where everything is so dear.
Buy your goods at the airport
And pay double, I fear.

Travellators take me from
Point A to point B.
I pass lounges and smoking zones.
Terminals One, Two and Three.

It's not the destination
But the journey we're on.
Sitting, eating or moving,
I try to sing my own song:

That each moment is precious.
I keep a smile on my face
As I stay present right now,
And move this body with grace.

I've lost count today –
Maybe six times I've felt
That bags, coats and tablets are
In trays on conveyor belts.

These days we're all screened.
Each is seen as a threat.
The bodies and belongings
Are all carefully checked.

It's hard to believe that
We once jumped on a plane
Back in the 70s and 80s,
When life seemed more sane.

jencompton.com

We've sure lost our innocence,
And some vile acts have been done
When we've harmed ourselves and others
With knife, bomb or gun.

So now, here's the test:
My flight to Spokane
Has been delayed two hours.
I'll **be** calm. Yes, I can.

'Cause I'm here and I'm breathing,
Doesn't matter so much where.
What counts in this moment
Is that I'm kind and I'm fair.

Somehow I'm connected
To all these people I see,
Who want to **be** happy.
Yep. They're just like me.

Please bless all these beings
Who are with me today.
May they all arrive safely,
Just like me, I do pray.

Just because you have baggage doesn't mean you have to lug it around.
– Richie Norton

The Flesh

- sweet and delicious

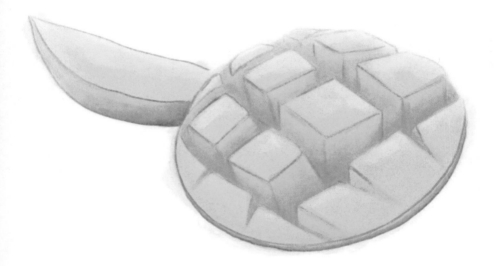

These poems deal with the stuff in life we love the most. We don't have to try to enjoy it. It tastes good. It feels right. It's rewarding. It's so easy to be here.

Life's a Mango

Can life **be** more perfect
Than a mango you think?
Sucking flesh and seed,
Standing at kitchen sink.

I'm totally here,
I'm totally **now**.
The taste of the mango
Says, OMG. Pow!

I stand at the sink,
The juice dripping down.
Mango becomes me;
The feeling's profound.

It demands to be noticed.
Blissed out. I'm here.
No past or future,
No pain and no fear.

I can't quite believe it.
Actually healthy!
This divine flavour
Has me feeling wealthy.

Be with each moment,
Like you are with this fruit.
So much in love now,
Not in constant pursuit.

Taste buds on fire.
I am now my tongue.
No arms, legs or body.
I'm ageless. I'm young!

This mango moment,
In your mouth today.
The joy and pleasure
Make you want to say,

Thank you for this.
Thank you for taste.
Give thanks for each second.
Not a moment to waste.

Life *is* a mango;
It's rich and it's here.
Savour the moment, and
You'll have no fear.

Life is like a mango.
– Brendan Pérez Compton

Nature

When you look at something
Like a tree or a bird,
Why don't you pretend
That you don't know the word?

Look at the thing and say,
Wow! What is that?
Pretend you don't know
That thing is called *cat*.

Take it all in with
Your eyes and your ears,
But now drop the label
And the image is clear.

That *thing* is a mystery
And so now are you.
Amazing, wonderful,
Believe me, it's true!

The words are just symbols
For the world that we know.
You can't understand,
For that, you must go –

To your heart, to your body,
To your eyes, ears and nose.
Get rid of the labels.
See how nature glows!

Sense nature just like
You do with a loved one.
Feel the connection
Like heat from the sun.

Wisdom begins in wonder.
– Socrates

First Thing in the Morning

When you become conscious
First thing in the day,
Does your mind start to move
Like a puppy at play?

It wants to run here,
Going this way and that.
You can't keep it still;
It just wants to react.

Your body's in bed,
But your mind's travelled far
From the past to the future,
From this planet to star.

Put a leash on this puppy,
And calm it right down.
Bring it back to the bed
Where the body is found.

Tell the mind it can wait.
Stop the travel in thought.
Keep your eyes closed, and
You sure won't get caught.

Bring your attention
To the sounds you can hear;
The birds and the cars,
The talk that is near.

Just stop the mind racing,
And tell it to wait.
Be with your body;
The feeling is great.

When you stop the machine
That is raring to go,
You become more relaxed,
And your body will know.

Once you're at peace,
Now you can arise.
Give thanks for the day,
And the fact you're alive.

Walk to the bathroom,
One step as you go.
Keep your mind on your feet,
Keep your mind way down low.

Tomorrow when you open
Your eyes and can see,
Stop the mind from racing.
Be still like a tree.

Notice your breath
As it moves in and out.
Feel the body in bed,
And there is no doubt

That your day will **be**
Calmer, wiser and clean.
Be aware of your senses,
And you'll see what I mean.

Life is the dancer, and you are the dance.
– Eckhart Tolle

A Love Journey

Have spent days going
Through albums of mum's life.
As child, friend and sister,
Daughter, mother and wife.

How good for the soul
To see mum in this way –
All the moments she's lived,
All the roles she does play.

Her kindness comes through
On the face that she has
With the people she loves,
With husband, her Baz.

She's kept friends from childhood
And made more on the way.
Giving and listening
Are what make her day.

What mum most loves is to
Be of service to us.
She'll do all in her power
Without too much fuss.

She excels with the planning.
She can run the show.
Attention to detail,
Her secret, you know.

She can type, garden, knit.
She can golf, bowl and cook.
She's travelled the world.
When will she write her book?

She knows how to listen.
It's us that she serves.
Uses all her talents.
This fine life she deserves.

She understands people.
She knows what makes you tick.
She's a sensitive being,
Will avoid the conflict.

She is a peacemaker.
Doesn't like us to fight.
Tries to bring us together,
To do what is right.

She's generous with money
And generous with time.
Goes to great lengths to please us
And make us feel fine.

She knows what makes you happy.
She'll do all that she can
To make it come true.
It's all part of her plan.

There's really nothing
That she can't do.
She's one talented lady.
She will surprise you.

She's patient, she's kind.
She knows when to be quiet.
Allows others their space,
Makes up her daily diet.

Each day is a chance
For her to do her best.
Makes lists of jobs
Before she can rest.

Mum, you're our queen.
You're our head of state.
We love and respect you.
How lucky our fate.

We've learned so much from you,
To stay positive and kind.
Such a great role model.
Praise, hope you don't mind.

When we think of you
Our heart becomes bright.
Having you in our life
Has shown us the light.

You inspire us all
To make the most of our time.
The journey you've taken
Has been simply sublime.

You're always right there
When we need you most.
From family who love you,
To you mum – a toast!

*My mother when
she was a child.*

All that I am or hope to be, I owe to my mother.
– Abraham Lincoln

Gratefulness

Can your eyes see words?
It's pretty amazing.
So lucky to have eyes
That we use for gazing.

Take them for granted?
Or do you think *wowee*!
These forms all around,
I can actually see!

Every moment you live
Is a chance to **be** grateful
For your senses, your life,
Your friends, your plateful!

When you live in this way,
You start to awaken.
No more will you live
Life as mistaken.

Your heart, it will open;
You give thanks for The Now.
This moment is precious,
And you will see how.

Your life, it will change;
You're more consciously here.
As your gratitude grows
For things you endear.

Opportunities come
As you start to feel
A generosity;
You'll share your next meal!

This moment **now**
However it looks,
Is a chance to **be** thankful.
You can't find it in books.

You just have a sense
Of wonder and awe
As you leave your house,
And walk out the door.

The trees and the birds,
The sky and the cloud,
Take a second to stop,
And say right out loud:

Thank you for this.
I'm connected to all.
So grateful for now,
I do not need more.

Even when this life
May hand you a lemon,
You just make lemonade,
And you'll **be** in heaven.

Take time to stop.
Be aware of this moment.
A gift you've been given;
It's not your opponent.

As water comes out from
The tap in the kitchen,
The light switch goes on
Or you start the ignition,

Say, *thank you for this.*
Don't take it for granted.
I'll celebrate **now**.
It's what I've been handed.

When reaching for bread,
Some jam or some honey,
Give thanks for those beings.
It's not all about money!

So many beings
Have worked hard for you.
So next time you eat,
Think as you chew –

How grateful I am
For the kindness of others.
They gave up their lives;
My sisters and brothers.

Gratitude is the sign of noble souls.
– Aesop

This Moment

This moment **now**:
An opportunity waiting.
Welcome it in,
And feel the vibrating.

Wherever you are
Get rid of the *should*.
Accept what is here,
And rejoice in the good.

When you get up to walk
From here to the next room,
Take each step on purpose
With your mind well in tune.

If you open the fridge,
Do it slowly with care.
Pick up the bottle, and
Really feel the glass there.

Can you hear the birds chirping?
Or the cars going past?
Be still in this moment;
You know it won't last.

When we are aware
Of each moment that is,
This life is more precious,
And not lived in a tizz.

Be as you wish to seem.
— Socrates

Your Dog

You come home from work
As tired as can be.
Your four-legged friend
You is happy to see.

He wags his tail,
Licks you on the face.
Incredible really,
This greeting is ace!

A dog doesn't judge you
Or think you're a jerk.
She just loves you a lot;
She'll stay when you're hurt.

You can see why we say
He is man's best friend;
No matter what happens,
He's there to the end.

You're out for an hour
Or maybe the day.
The greeting's the same:
She's willing to play.

What can he teach us
This friendly canine?
More joy and connection;
Everyone would feel fine.

When you walk in the door
She's not watching TV.
She barks and jumps up;
Fills you all with glee.

No sulking or temper,
No anger, resent.
She's right in the moment;
Fully now and present.

Imagine if we
Could live life this way.
People would feel loved,
All through the day.

Greet people you know
As if you're their pet!
No licking or jumping,
Just happiness get.

You can't wag your tail
Or lick them on the face,
But you can **be** joyful,
And feel full of grace.

So next time you see
Someone that you know,
Remember this poem,
And watch their heart glow.

jencompton.com

Smile warm and **be** pleased.
Let your body relax.
Look at them special.
Give them your max.

You will make their day
By greeting them such.
Think of that dog
Who loves you so much.

Be present right now.
Make your eyes wag.
Walk up to them smiling,
Don't feel like a dag.

It's so great to see you!
And make your face bright.
Remember your dog.
By George, he's so right.

Those who teach the most about humanity, aren't always humans.
– Donald L. Hicks

Thank You ABC

A is for air,
Allows me to breathe.
B is for the breath,
Which comes with such ease.

C is for creating,
The joy you have found.
D is for daybreak;
The bird's chirping sound.

E is for the earth,
On which our feet tread.
F is for the food;
Thanks for our daily bread.

G is for gratitude.
Give thanks for this day.
H is for the heart,
Which allows us to pray.

I is for *I am,*
The essence within.
J is for joy,
The life we've been given.

K is for knowing
That all will be well.
L is for learning
In this moment we dwell.

M is for memories,
Where we can go to.
N is for nature,
Her stillness in you.

O is for others;
All beings on Earth.
P is for our practice;
Each day a new birth.

Q is for questions;
To seek and to grow.
R is for resources,
Which allow life to flow.

S is for senses,
To embrace everything.
T is for the time to
Each day go within.

U is for union
With all that we see.
V is for vision
Of where we will **be**.

W is for water,
Which keeps us alive.
X is for xylitol,
Which is sweet, saves the hive.

Y is for you
Whom I value so much.
Z is for zestful,
For each life that we touch.

The root of joy is gratefulness.
– Brother David Steindl-Rast

Strangers

Most mornings I walk
Along a path by the creek.
The trees, air, the birds;
Is all that I seek.

As I walk, I'm mindful
Of my feet touching the ground,
Of my breath going in
And my ears hearing sound.

It's the best part of my day
As I give thanks for The Now.
So lucky to live here,
The mind always says, *Wow!*

Have been saying *hello*
To all the same faces
For thirteen years now;
My face theirs embraces.

I imagine their life,
Their house and their job,
Their longings and passions;
I wonder what makes them sob?

There is one man,
Our eyes always lock.
Could be something more;
But the boat we'll not rock.

Then the thin lady
Who walks oh so slow.
Gives me a faint smile,
And then on she does go.

There's a fat man in red
Who never wears shoes.
His face is so kind.
I wonder his views.

There's a trio of three
Who walk and they gossip.
One might make eye contact,
I wish they would stop it.

There are people with dogs,
There are people who run,
Both men and women
Out under the sun.

It's kind of relaxing
To not have to talk.
To smile, to acknowledge
And then on I do walk.

Today passed a woman
Who talked on her phone.
Face was angry, uptight;
She should have left it at home.

That's the whole point
Of connecting with trees;
To escape from the gadgets
And sense how it frees.

If we don't take some time
To relax, go within then
Our lives become hectic;
Just one crazy spin.

Step out of this century
And go back in time;
Spend moments connecting
With nature – sublime.

Not all those who wander are lost.
– J.R.R. Tolkien

Your Dream

He's studying so hard
At acting, his craft.
Reads novels and scripts
All day; it's his path.

He's right in the moment.
That's just how he is.
Doesn't care for mundane;
He's all for showbiz.

He's showing me how
I could live this life
By being creative,
More than mother and wife.

We all have these talents
That we keep tucked away.
Let them come out, **be** seen
For they need to play.

They want to work through us;
To bring light into the world.
We sometimes ignore them
Whether we're boy or girl.

Let your light shine now.
Create and **be** seen.
Do what you love, and
Dare to have the big dream.

You won't regret it;
You'll be true to yourself.
Your gifts and your talent
Bring you inner wealth.

My son, he has taught me
To follow my dream.
Be bold, **be** creative;
Do what makes you keen.

When we live life this way
Then we so feel alive.
Connected to others,
It gives us the drive

To keep going on,
To get out of bed.
You follow your dream
Knowing you will be led.

On a meaningful journey
Of wonder and light.
There will be some hitches,
But don't give up the fight.

If you've got talent
That needs to be shown,
Stop making excuses.
Get it out there! Get known!

You go to some market;
You're buying their art.
That's not what you need now.
Find your gift. Now start!

Don't say, *Not creative,*
I'm no good at this.
Let the idea take hold
And it do not dismiss.

Every day do a bit
Of the art that you love.
It will start to take flight
Like some pure, white dove.

No matter your age,
Your status or role,
Give an hour or so
Each day to your goal.

Don't be dramatic,
Get angry or curse.
Just keep plugging at it.
You'll get better, not worse.

The secret is to
Be committed to art.
Wake up early each day
And make a good start.

You still do your day job
So you can pay the bill,
But your art form evolves
'Cause you have the will.

Don't expect to be rich
Or seek out the fame.
Do your best each day,
And life won't be the same.

The joy it will grow
In leaps and in bounds.
Your treasure you've opened,
A secret you've found.

Be brave, do it now.
Start ideas in motion.
You'll transform yourself;
It's your magic potion.

Go confidently in the direction of your dreams! Live the life you've imagined.
– Henry David Thoreau

Kindness

I look at my workmate.
What do I see?
A brother? A sister?
They are just like me.

They want to be happy,
To feel safe and good.
I could be them.
Have I understood?

Nobody's perfect.
We have good days and bad.
If someone is nasty
It's 'cause inside they're sad.

Be kind to this person
'Cause they could be you.
And you're never quite sure
What some have been through.

Look through the anger
And the mean words.
Ask, *Are you ok?*
It's not so absurd.

Be still and relaxed,
Forgive them I must.
I keep being kind,
I will win their trust.

For no one is perfect,
And least of all me.
I too have my faults,
Which others can see.

Be kind to your mates.
Just think of them first.
You'll see the rewards
As you start to rehearse.

No act of kindness, no matter how small, is ever wasted.
– Aesop

Another Birthday

Years say you're eighty-
Something and I'm fifty-five.
I think we're just grateful
To both be alive!

Not all beings on earth
Get to live for so long.
Their life is cut short.
Who knows? Right or wrong.

We may live a day more
Or maybe there's ten.
Not the number of days,
But the times we call *friend*.

When our heart opens,
When it sees others as me,
When we give with love
To all creatures, we see.

May your birthday **be** bright
As you give thanks for this life.
A memorable journey
And one very good wife.

You've been blessed with so much,
And you've given back too.
Keep living and loving
To all those who know you.

Do not let making a living prevent you from making a life.
– John Wooden

Praise

Some people give out praise
Like they're handing out gold.
They'd rather see bad,
Speak frank or then scold.

Someone says, *You're no good,*
Hopeless or useless.
Do you want to go on?
What's the point? It's fruitless.

Let's say there's something
That you want to try:
A hobby or a sport.
You spend money and buy.

If your teacher can see
You've got what it takes,
They'll encourage you now.
Success is what makes.

When we praise from the heart,
The other can hear.
They want to excel.
They let go of the fear.

Use words that imply
They simply can't fail.
It fills them with strength;
Confidence will prevail.

Keep your face bright,
Keep your language clean.
They'll keep getting better.
You'll see what I mean.

If they are struggling
Or there is a hitch,
Tell them they'll make it;
Their pride you'll enrich.

When you convince someone
That they are a winner,
That's half the battle,
Their face is a grinner.

Don't punish or force.
Don't threaten, cajole.
Keep praising their efforts;
Know this is your role.

Some of the greats,
Like Dickens and Wells,
Received praise by others,
And so their book sells.

If you're sincere and
Use praise as a tool,
What you give to loved ones
Is like rocket fuel.

They'll start to take off.
Wow! Look at them go.
Upwards and onwards.
From your praise it will flow.

The transformation
Is just so exciting.
Encourage someone, like
Fireworks igniting.

Takes kindness and wisdom
To watch someone flower.
Your attitude and words
Will them empower.

Stand back and just watch.
You're the wind beneath wings.
Your praise and your love;
The canary now sings.

When we tell them they can,
They believe in themself.
Nothing will stop them;
They work like Santa's elf!

If there's someone you love
Then show it this way.
Use words of praise, and
Believe what you say.

I praise loudly. I blame softly.
– Catherine the Great

Stillness

Really look at a flower,
A plant or a tree.
It says, *I am as I am*
With such dignity.

It doesn't pretend
To **be** something it's not.
It endures all weathers,
Staying in the same spot.

It's something so sacred,
The natural world.
It reminds us that we too
Need to stop the great whirl.

What can I learn
From this regal display that
Doesn't try to be different
Night time and day?

Maybe we too
Just need to **be**
At one with our essence,
And then we shall see.

To rejoice in the moment,
Whatever it takes:
From hailstones to sunshine,
From rain to snowflakes.

Nature doesn't complain.
It just lives on,
Adapting to conditions,
Which make it so strong.

What if we too then
Accepted our lot,
Not resisting all,
Learning best when to stop?

Nature is **here**.
It's not past or future.
Its temporary form
Does not create stupor.

It rejoices in **now**,
Accepts the form it takes.
Jacarandas don't long
To be like great lakes.

I am who I am.
Look at nature as teacher.
Its presence, its stillness
Really is the best preacher.

So the next time
I look at a plant or a tree,
I'll connect with its essence,
Which is also with me.

Adopt the pace of nature: her secret is patience.
– Ralph Waldo Emerson

Consciousness

This is a word which
Is quite hard to say.
Con-shus-ness is
How you say it today.

So what is this thing
Which we will call IT?
IT is your awareness,
Your presence. You're IT!

When you are asleep
You can't sense IT at all.
But when you wake up,
IT comes back to your call.

There are five ways that IT
Lets us know that IT's there.
Feel these right now,
Right **now** if you dare.

Sense the eyes that can see,
Sense the ears that can hear,
Sense the tongue that can taste,
And the nose smells what is near.

Your skin, it can feel.
Be aware of this thing.
Your mind will stop thinking;
The space will begin.

Look without labelling.
You hear a bell ring.
You touch your hand.
You taste anything.

You smell that food cooking.
You look up at a star.
Your consciousness working;
That is who **you** are.

Say goodbye to your thoughts.
To your senses you go.
This will help you focus,
To **be** with the flow.

Consciousness is
Such a wonderful link
To our beautiful world,
And you don't need to think.

I am conscious, therefore I am.
– Eckhart Tolle

Your Heart

What is your heart?
Let's take a good look.
Does it just pump blood
From the head to the foot?

The heart is more
Like that of a brain.
An intelligence, yes
That truly does reign.

Unlike the brain,
Too clever for good,
The heart we can trust.
That is understood.

You do have to think,
Use your brain every day,
But **be** guided by the heart
Whilst working for pay.

The thoughts want attention.
Say, *Hey, look at me!*
We can't hear the heart.
Too noisy, just **be**.

Your heart does not lie.
It always speaks true.
Listen, just listen;
It's guidance for you.

Breathe with the heart.
Breathe in and breathe out.
Put your hands on your chest;
Feel connection throughout.

You see our true path,
The way we must tread,
Is found in our heart
And not in our head.

We're experts at telling
The heart to be quiet.
The brain and the thoughts,
Are our daily diet.

Your heart will connect you
To nature and me,
To all forms of life;
From earthworm to tree.

If everyone around you
Says, *Sit down, it's clear!*
But your heart says, *Stand,*
Then do that my dear!

Be still and listen.
Come down to your heart.
Trust what it says.
It really is smart.

jencompton.com

Smart in a way
That goes beyond thought,
A beautiful wisdom
That cannot be taught.

You won't find it in
Schools, unis or books.
Each living thing has it:
A pig and a chook.

Take time every day
To connect within.
Acknowledge your heart;
Its trust you will win.

It will never lie
Nor do you wrong.
It is your best guide
For which you so long.

Your compassion will grow,
You'll feel more at ease,
Problems decrease now.
There'll be less disease.

Heart shines with all beauty
And radiates out,
Wisdom and knowing
Leave little doubt.

The pain and the aches,
The good days and bad,
Give thanks for your heart,
A full well that is glad.

Please love your heart
'Cause it surely loves you.
Learn how to trust now.
Your heart will see you through.

The longest journey you will make in your life is from your head to your heart.
– Sioux Indians

Hot Chips and Lemonade

Hey, have you realised
That now you are making
The memories for your kids;
That's what you're creating.

Lighten up now and
Don't be so stern.
Just 'cause you're adult
Doesn't mean you can't learn.

Today, ask your kids
What they'd like to do.
Whatever the answer,
Well, make it come true!

No strict analysis
Of nutritional worth.
Let go of the rules;
It's a memory birth.

Let's ride to the park!
Hot chips and lemonade!
Be like a wizard;
Their day you have made.

They can't quite believe
That you've dropped your guard.
They'll go with the flow though,
Run around in the yard.

When I was a kid:
Ice blocks before breakfast;
A treat from my nana,
It felt truly reckless.

My nan she did ask us
If mum would approve.
We'd nod our heads slowly
So she would conclude.

Rules and more rules seem
To dictate our life.
Let go for a while,
Dance with your wife!

Be like a kid and
Laugh. Have some fun.
Your kids love to see you
Out there in the sun.

jencompton.com

No need for the drink,
The telly or phone.
When you love this moment,
You're right in the zone.

Sometimes we get trapped
By being adult.
Life gets so serious.
Kids may want to bolt.

They don't need the lectures,
The constant advice.
They just want to see you;
Boy, that sure feels nice.

Relax in the moment
And treasure this time
That you spend with the kids.
You know, it's sublime.

Every moment you share
That is bright and true,
Is a memory for them
That will carry them through.

When they have tough days
They'll go back to the past.
Look what you've given;
A gift that will last.

So, go break the rules.
Give them a great treat.
Laugh and **be** present;
You're making life sweet.

Every time you invest
In this special moment,
The returns, they will come;
They have no opponent.

A happy life **now**
Is a happy life past.
Reach out to your kids.
This is real, not a draft.

Children are like wet cement. Whatever falls on them makes an impression.
– Dr. Hiam Ginnot

La Sierra de Francia

When I write a poem,
I need to feel inspired.
A deep feeling comes up;
I know it's desired.

For thirty years now
I've been in love with a place.
Its valleys, rivers and trees,
Quaint pueblos with grace.

The sound of the leaves
As they rustle in the breeze,
The chestnuts, the oaks,
The pine trees; they please.

There's nowhere on earth
That smells so divine.
I take lots of full breaths,
So content. I feel fine.

The air and the water;
It's fresh and it's clean.
Wellbeing and joy
Flood my senses. Serene.

When we swim in the rivers,
The water tastes sweet.
The sun on my skin –
I'm alive. I'm complete.

A life that feels simple,
A life that is clean.
Fruit trees and oak trees,
Las jaras; supreme.

The rocks are so smooth
On my feet in the sun.
I hear the river flowing.
A better feeling? There's none.

There are plenty of trees
That I now know the name –
Los nogales, los castaños,
Los manzanos, the same.

Walks on the pebble tracks
With pine trees around.
Saw a male goat who ran
Through the trees; not a sound.

There's nowhere on earth
That I love more than here.
La Alberca, Las Batuecas,
To my eyes bring a tear.

It's like I am one
With the sky and the air,
The trees and the mountains;
I'm young without care.

jencompton.com

The vultures, they soar.
The swallows, they flit.
The blue sky's so intense;
From its cup I do sip.

There are speckled brown eagles,
There are hawks that do glide;
Beautiful birds that no doubt
Make a lamb want to hide.

The food tastes so good;
Olives, cheese and cold beer.
Life feels so perfect.
Every moment is dear.

Gracias querida Castilla
For your people and places.
My heart is so grateful
For this land it embraces.

The mountains are calling and I must go.
– John Muir

Places from the Past

The place where you played,
The place where you grew,
Lives in your heart;
It becomes part of you.

It may be the sea,
A river or creek,
Mountains or fields,
A park near your street.

The place takes on
A life of its own.
It brings back memories
Of where we have grown.

For me, it's the sea,
The sand and the rocks.
Sound of waves lapping
Where the yacht docks.

What about you?
What place is so dear
That when you go back
Your heart does endear?

I walk on the beach
And a feeling arises;
A deep kind of knowing,
Holds many surprises.

Hard to explain;
Once took it for granted.
Now with grown eyes,
It all looks enchanted.

As I take each step,
A memory will come.
A moment from the past;
My dad and my mum.

King tides in the summer,
Rows on the bay,
Goggles and flippers,
Swimming all day.

A feeling comes up of
Being part of this scene.
My cells and this place
Are one that have been.

Different version of me
Going out in the boat,
With a man I shared life with,
Who's now so remote.

The days that I spent
Growing up here
Have moulded my nature.
I do hold them dear.

The westerly winds
And southerly buster.
White horses on bay
In storm time do muster.

The places I visit
And that I once knew,
Look and feel different
To me than to you.

jencompton.com

To somebody else
It's just a street or a place.
Nothing special to them,
But to you it holds grace.

Place touches our heart
With the child that's within.
Not just a field or a beach.
It may bring a grin.

It's like when you hear
A song that you know;
It transports you back years
To a place or a beau.

The form of the site
Brings up an emotion;
May be happy or sad,
Like some magic potion.

Just talking about
That place from the past,
Gives you a strange feeling;
A spell it does cast.

Laps at the rock pools,
Walks along esplanade,
Sitting at look-outs
On sandstone that's hard.

No matter the age
That life says you are,
A memory appears and
You travel back far.

Be grateful for places
And the memories they hold.
When you go back there, greet
An old friend; she's gold.

We do not remember days, we remember moments.
– Cesare Pavese

Come out of the Head

Come out of the head,
Move into the heart.
Be aware of your breath,
Come on! Let's make a start.

Feel your presence,
Feel it within.
This is the place
Where you must begin.

Just **be** with it **now**.
Don't think, just **be** still.
This is your essence;
There's no need to will.

Sense your face, your ears,
Your neck and your chest.
Go down through the body
Until your feet, you do rest.

Try this each day
Whenever you walk,
In a place where it's quiet,
Where there's no one who'll talk.

Also when sitting,
Lying or flat.
Gets you out of your head.
It will bring you back.

Life has taught me to think, but thinking has not taught me to live.
– Alexander Herzen

jencompton.com

Confidence

What is confidence?
How does it look?
Do you have to be rich?
Perhaps written a book?

Does confidence come
From your charm? Your wit?
The houses you own?
Are you friends with Brad Pitt?

Perhaps you have beauty
Or you're well educated.
Are you a famous *someone*
And more elevated?

None of these factors
Give us what we seek,
For confidence is something
That comes from so deep.

It radiates out,
An invisible sun.
Its warm presence is
Felt by all, everyone.

Confidence is something
That cannot be taught.
A wise, deep essence
Of love that shines forth.

There's no more fear.
There's no worry or shame.
You see we're connected.
Who needs all the fame?

To others you may
Seem quiet or odd,
But they do not know
Your essence is God.

You feel without doubt
You're connected to all.
This deep conscious knowing
Is the ego's downfall.

You accept who you are.
You embrace all the others.
You see beyond form;
They're your sisters and brothers.

Others may want it.
They're not sure who you are.
You're nobody special,
Yet you have come so far.

This confidence comes
Saying *yes* to The Now.
It goes beyond self
And brings peace somehow.

There's no more worry.
You no longer compare
Yourself to your neighbour
Or someone out there.

You just enjoy **be**ing
'Cause that is enough.
There's no need for extras;
All that fancy stuff.

So **be** content with
The one who you are.
Feel the presence within.
Shine forth like a star.

The challenge is not to be perfect, it's to be whole.
– Jane Fonda

Lucky Duck

This is a true story
About a pet duck.
Talk about karma,
She sure had good luck!

Her mother has twelve,
She is one of those.
Takes ducklings across street
But Daisy, she knows.

She just would not follow
Her mum to the creek.
She sat down on the path.
She was tiny and weak.

My friend, Helen,
Saw the whole thing.
She picked up this duck and
To her home she did bring.

The reason she took her
Was because of the eels.
They love baby ducklings,
It's one of their favourite meals.

Of the twelve ducklings,
Just five now were left.
Helen went to the creek,
And she felt so bereft.

Daisy now has a home
And lives on the bay.
She loves to go swimming,
And would do it all day.

Helen has bought her
A small wading pool.
She can waddle down ramp
But she's stubborn as a mule.

One day Helen took Daisy
To the RSL Club.
She popped head from the basket,
And a man dropped his sub.

He went to complain
To the club's boss,
Who told him that Daisy
Was welcome, no loss.

Once Helen was quietly
Watching TV at night.
Daisy flew across the room,
And gave her a big fright.

Her wings must be clipped
So she can't fly away,
For she'd die with no
Mum-model. Yes, she must stay.

Helen clipped off her wings.
It made her feel sad,
But Daisy was a pet now,
And her life wasn't bad.

She's one lucky duck
Living there on the bay.
There are greyhounds next door
So she's wary at play.

Helen will not kill her
Nor fatten her up.
No way she would eat her
With orange for supp.

Daisy nuzzles her neck
To show her she cares.
Talks with her eyes saying,
Get me down off this chair!

Helen's bought her a pram
Where Daisy can sit.
She can push her along,
Daisy has fun for a bit.

Pigs, ducks and cows
Are beautiful beasts.
When we give them a name,
On them could not feast.

Remember Charlotte?
She wrote words in her web,
So Wilbur the pig
Would not end up dead.

All mammals are social.
You can make them your pet.
They will return love to
Your heart, if you them let.

People eat pigs and ducks,
Cats and dogs we name *pet*
But reverse could be true
If our culture would let.

This is the true story
Of lovely white Daisy,
Whose life was transformed
Because she was lazy!

Nature teaches beasts to know their friends.
– William Shakespeare

Creative Trust

Wherever you are **now**,
Whatever you do,
Stay curious, alert.
Let this life guide you.

As in a treasure hunt,
Start looking for clues.
They are like signposts.
You have nothing to lose.

Be light, **be** playful.
Remember Bugs Bunny?
Nothing too serious.
We laughed. He was funny.

Sometimes we think that
Life has to be dark.
Rigid. Painful.
Life loses its spark.

Do you do tragedy?
Need to suffer each day?
It's really not worth it;
It's a crime; doesn't pay.

Be in wonder **now**,
Bring out the inner child.
Your first Christmas lights.
Amazed! Laugh out loud.

The people you meet,
The things that you see.
Be delighted, in awe.
Just set your heart free.

Be open to life.
Be part of its flow.
Look, Feel and Listen.
Who knows where you'll go!

Although you create,
You don't need to suffer.
Be glad, **be** grateful.
Come, trust now you duffer.

Look and learn from the birds,
Delight in the day.
Nature loves life;
No resistance, fair play.

Be like the joker.
I love getting that card.
Look what he can do.
He's magic, not scarred.

Try not to label
What you find on the hunt.
No good and no bad now.
My best pet was a runt.

The trick is to engage
With people and life.
You believe in giving,
In the process. Less strife.

Drop the attachment
To the art you create.
Stay in love with your work.
It may change, it's your fate.

Let your heart **be** bright.
Hold things light as sand.
You trust in the journey;
Who knows where you'll land?

Passion and tragic.
Martyr and pain.
Let it all go 'cause
You've got nothing to gain.

Whatever you're doing,
Look around and **be** glad.
Always something amazing.
Be grateful, not sad.

Stay curious, alive
Like in our travels
To lands far away, and
Just see what unravels.

Go get *Big Magic*.
It's a wonderful read.
Changes how you create;
It will plant the seed.

When you make your art
Or start with your book,
Be ready for changes.
Be *Brave Heart* not *Sook*.

Put your money on *bright*,
On *positive* and *joy*.
They add glitter to life.
What a picture. Oh boy!

The chief enemy of creativity is 'good' sense.
– Pablo Picasso

Just be Present

Just **be** present, and
Be present **now.**
Drop thoughts of the past.
Come back to The Now.

The future's not real;
Just a thought in your head.
If you dwell on it much,
You really will dread.

Come back to The Now
'Cause it's all that is real.
This wonderful moment,
To **be** and just feel.

When you find yourself
Drifting forward or back,
Pinch yourself on the arm,
Or give it a smack.

Come back to the present.
Be present **now.**
It's a gift just for you,
If you merely allow.

It is better to travel well than to arrive.
– Shakyamuni Buddha

This Precious Life

Each of us has
A most precious thing:
The life force inside us.
It has a nice ring!

Unless we are *thinking*,
We don't feel we're alive.
But this is not true;
It's by far a big lie.

We may not yet know
To **be** alive is to **be**,
When gazing at something
Like a lamp or a tree.

This is the place where
We truly belong.
This stillness and presence
Is The one true song,

That we must sing
If we are to survive,
To live life with joy,
To grow and to thrive.

Whatever you do,
Wherever you are,
Be totally present;
You'll feel best by far.

Stop thinking! Stop thinking!
Come back to right here.
Where are you now?
Stay with it. **Be** clear.

Give to this moment
Like you give to a baby.
Love it and sense it,
Be grateful then maybe,

Your life will improve.
You'll stop searching for more.
You'll soon come to see that
Desire is poor.

Be content with The Now,
And welcome it in.
Others will feel it
And give you a grin.

This is the path on
Which you must tread.
Be aware and awake,
Not caught up in your head.

When you are truly in love with life, every breath you take is gratitude.
– Bryant McGill

The Horse Whisperer

I've known her as a teacher;
Intuitive and kind.
She's done retail and sales.
Can Do approach in her mind.

Northern beaches in Sydney,
She grew up near the sand,
But she said to her guy,
Let's drive to Queensland!

Found five acres on a hill
With a view to die for.
Had a vision of future,
A life to explore.

Her name's Catriona
And she lives on a farm
With husband and animals.
Let me tell you her yarn:

Spectacular views of
Mountains and fields,
Grass and trees.
Her home really appeals.

Avocados and lemons,
Macadamias and more.
So much to take in,
So much land to explore.

Pablo and Bella,
Each *one* has a name.
Dogs, horses and chickens,
He/she finds shelter from rain.

She puts on her gumboots
And walks around the yard,
Feeding and cleaning,
Collecting; it's hard.

At the end of the day
'Cause she's always on the go,
Likes a Canadian Club
Or a Pinot Grigio.

So much to do,
But she loves it, oh yeah!
Knows each animal's soul,
And she tries to be fair.

Tara, she rides often so
She can keep the peace 'cause
This mare's jealous of new ones
And acts funny, retreats.

There's the frisky new foal
Who got bashed on the head,
And the pony she rescued,
Who would probably be dead.

Just like nature takes time
But accomplishes things,
With horses she trains and
Sees what patience, it brings.

This woman is tough,
She's confident and strong,
But she'll cry in a second
If a being is wronged.

She can get horses to do
All manner of things,
'Cause she's firm but forgiving
As she moulds nature, love brings.

This Sydney girl's heart
Is as vast as the ocean.
Wants to care and protect
Like a calm, healing lotion.

Her husband and children
Come first, yes, siree
But there's room in her heart
For more than just three.

She's created a haven
For all who are living.
There's love and more love
From this soul who's so giving.

What she wants most
Is to share all her wealth
With those whom she loves;
Food, shelter, good health.

When she whispers to her horses,
There's a change in her face.
She so *gets* who they are,
They trust her. She's Ace.

She competes in horse shows;
Goes all dressed up in white.
Struts, jumps and parades.
She and horse do alright.

This lady just loves to feel
Young and free on her ride;
Cantering through the bush
With good friend by her side.

They smile and they laugh
As they ride like the wind.
Nothing's better than this;
Ear to ear, a huge grin.

This land's in her blood.
There are no words that can say.
Wants to be here forever,
Till her dying day.

So many years of
Love and hard toil,
To bring this dream to fruition.
To this land, she is loyal.

She just can't imagine
Being anywhere but here.
This place and the animals,
To her heart are so dear.

What she has created
Is a heaven on earth.
A retreat and a haven;
Here, all beings have worth.

What this free spirit loves most
Is to **be** of service to all;
To see others content,
She picks them up when they fall.

Loves her man and her girls,
Her animals, the farm.
Cries buckets of tears
Should they come to harm.

Thank you, kind lady,
For your big, generous heart.
This world is so grateful
For the love you impart.

Until one has loved an animal, a part of one's soul remains unawakened.
– Anatole France

My Ode to Violet

It pierces my eyeballs;
The colour's intense.
As I walk or drive past,
My heart's joy feels immense.

I can't quite believe that
This tree is for real.
It's a natural wonder
And so grateful I feel

To live in a city
Where every October,
These trees line the streets
And just bowl me over.

The colour is lavender,
Violet, lilac or mauve.
It knocks your socks off
To see them in a grove.

It's my favourite colour,
So gorgeous I want to cry.
To think I've the merits
To see this before I die.

Originally from Brazil,
But it thrives here in Brisbane,
This gift from Mother Nature
Is the royal queen of tree kingdom.

Have you ever beheld something
That makes you want to cry?
Its beauty pierces your heart.
It's something money can't buy.

What are the chances
That I'd reside in a place,
With this purple rain,
Which brings beauty and grace.

If you're somewhere up high,
Wow! An incredible sight
To view this violet canopy
That to the eyes brings delight.

Not only the blossoms
When they're still on the tree,
But the lilac on green grass
Creates a blanket or sea.

jencompton.com

The blossoms fall to the ground
And there's a lavender cover;
A sea of purple that surely
Inspires artist and lover.

If this magnificent tree
Is near Flame Tree or Poinciana,
Oh my gosh! I assure you
There's no sight that is finer.

Each of the blossoms,
They all come together
To bring such intense splendour;
They're all birds of a feather.

I suppose you've guessed by now
The name of this tree.
First planted here in 1864;
It's called the Jacaranda Tree.

To get some really good photos,
Go to New Farm Park or UQ.
Will have you snapping like crazy,
This vivid violet hue.

My ode to the Jacaranda –
Your beauty blows me away.
May these eyes devour you again
One grey or sunny spring day.

Trees are poems that the earth writes upon the sky.
– Kahlil Gibran

The Seed

- impossible to digest

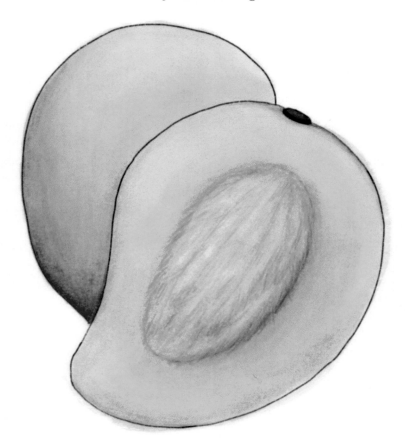

These poems deal with slightly dark themes and unpleasant situations. The experiences may not bring us happiness. They may make us uncomfortable or cause negative emotions to arise. Even so, if we learn from them and use them wisely, we can move forward to a better place.

The News on TV

The news on TV
Sometimes makes me sick.
I think it's astounding
The stories they pick.

Murders and robberies,
Homicides and evasion.
Why does the media
Decide on invasion?

If someone goes crazy
And shoots in a crowd,
You'll see it tonight
Because it's allowed.

But if there's a gathering
Of souls wanting change,
You may see a minute,
Then back to deranged.

Watching the news,
Night after night
Will make you depressed;
You may live in fright.

You'll see the world
As one scary place.
The reality of TV
Right there in your face.

Watch the news with caution.
Don't believe all you see.
The wise amongst us
Are very wary.

The media just want
An interesting story.
Something spectacular,
Strange, amazing or gory.

They want your emotions
To get really aroused,
Your opinions strengthened,
Your voice becomes loud.

You talk at the TV
So no one can listen.
They've sucked you right in,
They've completed their mission.

You totally believe
The media is true.
There's more to this story
Than they're showing you.

If you want to awaken
And feel calm and light,
Give the news a miss
When you come home tonight.

An eye for an eye only ends up making the whole world blind.
– Mahatma Gandhi

Watch Your Language

Pick up your socks and
Go clean your room.
Now, get dressed quickly;
They'll be here real soon.

This is the only talk
That some children hear.
Functional language that
Does not hold them dear.

These things must be said
For our lives to work,
But if it's all that you say,
Kids will go berserk.

Kids long to share time and
Hear words from the heart.
Go beyond the mundane;
Show their inner spark.

They want you to **be**
Your relaxed, normal self.
Drop the role of parent.
Give them your wealth.

Get rid of the ego,
Criticism and orders.
Just **be** with your child;
You'll see less disorders.

Allow their **be**ing to
Shine like a star.
Watch what you say.
Don't change who they are.

Get rid of how you
Think they *should* be.
To be critical is
Devastating you see.

They'll start to withdraw;
You'll see less and less.
I can't measure up.
In their mind they confess.

When you were a kid,
Your parents did it to you.
Now you're repeating
What before made you stew.

Go spend some time
In a park or the bush.
Make a vow not to
Speak critical or push.

Be relaxed, **be** yourself.
Give thanks for this child.
Let them see who you are,
Let go for a while.

When your child feels safe
To **be** who they are,
Less functional language,
There's no need to spar.

If you take the time
To show them your soul,
When you do give orders,
They'll then play the role.

You don't need to spend
A whole heap of money.
Accept who they are.
It won't feel that funny.

Just make them feel safe,
And laugh. Have some fun.
Don't make it harder
For the journey they're on.

They need your smiles,
Your presence, support.
If you're too critical,
Their love drops to nought.

The food that they need
Cannot be eaten.
Your encouragement and praise
Can never be beaten.

Be sure to taste your words before you spit them out.
– Auliq Ice

Feeling Hurt

Have you ever been hurt
By what somebody says?
You just can't forgive them.
Your anger, it spreads.

From your head to your feet,
Your stomach and chest.
You'll NEVER forgive them,
And you know the rest.

You avoid them, oh yes,
Tell others they're awful.
Throw darts at their photo,
Think thoughts unlawful.

The person you've decided
Is worse than a devil,
Is actually like you,
And now I will level.

They made a mistake.
They caused you some pain.
Your ego got wounded
And hurt, once again.

Close your eyes now and
Imagine they're here.
Sitting opposite you,
I know you feel fear.

You don't want to be there.
You're uncomfortable too,
But you need to ask them
To listen to you.

You get to tell them
All the things that they said,
That caused you such heartache,
That did in your head.

As you talk in your mind,
Your enemy listens.
The tears slowly trickle
Down their cheeks that glisten.

Now you must listen to
Their side of the story.
It's hard to at first;
You're not in your glory.

How can we people
Get things so wrong?
See it from their side,
You feel like a nong.

You tell them you're sorry
And they say so too.
You both feel awkward;
Want to start all anew.

jencompton.com

The pain starts to ease,
Your heart feels at peace.
You look in their eyes,
You see the release.

You just hadn't realised
The things that you said,
Had wounded them greatly.
They rejected instead.

It's easy to forget
The words that we say,
But when others wound us,
We can tell them the day!

Feel the peace now
In your heart and your chest.
The anger is going,
Your relief is the best.

Understanding the other
From their point of view,
Will help you forgive
Both themselves and you.

When you meet them for real
In the shopping mart,
Send them thoughts of kindness
Straight from your heart.

They can't help but feel this,
And feel this they must.
Then things will soften, and
There'll be more trust.

There's no need for words,
Just send them your kindness.
The healing's begun, put
An end to the blindness.

To have a friend, you have to Be a friend.
– Elbert Hubbard

Advice to a Father

His children come home,
And they long to be seen,
But he can't even take
His eyes off the screen.

The telly is a god.
It's where he most likes to be.
The beings around him,
He just cannot see.

He doesn't ask questions
Or say, *How are you?*
He doesn't say, *Hello,*
So, tell me, what's new?

He sits and he sits
In front of the screen,
Whilst his children grow up:
Five….twelve…seventeen.

He just doesn't realise
All the moments he misses.
These beautiful beings
Who are like joyful kisses.

When will he see that
The movies he views,
Cannot hide his
Communication issues?

How would he feel
When he walked in the house,
Nobody said *boo*,
Not even a mouse.

How can someone be
So rude and so cold?
Not talk to his children:
More precious than gold.

Wake up and enjoy the
People who care.
One day you'll feel sad
When they're no longer there.

A telly's not real;
It's just a projection,
But your children are **life**,
Don't need your rejection.

Be awake, **be** alert,
And see them with eyes.
If you don't change your ways,
They will you despise.

Be with your kids
Like you are with your dog,
Who lights up your eyes;
Brings you out of the fog.

Your kids are so precious.
They're alive and they're here.
Wake up silly man
Or you'll lose them I fear.

The hunger for love is much more difficult to remove than the hunger for bread.
– Mother Teresa

Are You Sure ?

You think they're the problem.
Are you sure that you're right?
Spend all day complaining;
Oh my, what a plight!

You have a vision
Of how they should behave.
Blame them for your misery?
It's you, you must save.

So, just their presence
Has you feeling uptight,
What they say, how they move;
You're ready to bite.

You've been with them so long,
You know how they'll react
To comments and questions,
To fiction and fact.

There's so much about them
That drives you insane.
Like a cracked record;
Here we go again!

Your karma has chosen
You both as a pair.
Make the most now and learn;
It's a test, don't despair.

Their thoughts about you?
Perhaps you would faint
To find out from them,
They don't see you as a saint.

Get rid of the blaming
And work on yourself.
Practise love and compassion;
You will feel its wealth.

See them as your project;
As a gift you have got.
Next time they say something,
Breathe. And then stop.

Now, you have a choice
Which path you will tread:
The old, painful one
Or the one with less dread.

Just watch that reaction,
Familiar play,
Look at it different;
Observe and delay.

Become the observer
Of what's going on.
Step out of yourself,
Guard your words before gone.

It's so easy to blame
Others for our pain,
But they are a mirror
So look, see and train.

Soon you will notice
The change in the air,
As you work on yourself
With love, not despair.

Switch reacting for listening,
Switch irritation for care.
See them as a patient;
Show your genuine care.

Relate to them now
From your heart not your head;
Your own experiment,
You're both alive and not dead.

All the advice you ever gave your partner is for you to hear.
– Byron Katie

Sickness

Your body, my body
Will one day get sick.
Could be a cold, flu,
A bite from a tick.

What if your sickness
Is really quite bad?
A tumour? A cancer?
That makes you so sad.

If you fret and worry,
Your mind loses control.
You think of the worst,
Go down the black hole.

You'll blame and you'll curse.
Not talk to another.
You're just so consumed.
The truth you do smother.

You become all obsessed
With your own sickness.
It's all you can see.
It's all you can witness.

Here's what to do if
You get really sick:
Accept the disease.
Try not to resist.

The cloud, it does have
A silver lining.
You can't see it now,
Because you are frowning.

Talk to your sickness
Like you talk to a friend,
Why are you here then?
Have you come to mend?

Sickness can take us
Where we'd never go.
Incredible journey –
Just go with the flow.

Don't see it as hostile,
Threatening or mean.
Use it to grow now.
Let the sickness **be** seen.

If you can see it
As friend and not foe,
You will suffer less.
Your spirit you'll know.

Be calm and **be** present.
Look inwards, not out.
Ask why you have this.
Choose wonder, not doubt,

Will come to you soon
In some kind of form.
A peace, a knowing
Will start to **be** born.

Nothing is as it
Appears now to be.
This sickness, disease,
It will set you free.

So many people
Have said and me too,
That sickness is a blessing,
Shines forth a new you.

Here's what will happen:
Your compassion will grow
For all the others,
Who you do not know.

You're not the only
One who has pain.
Billions of others
Like you, just the same.

Try to stop thinking,
Oh, poor little me!
Look at it different,
Your eyes then will see.

Disease is a blessing.
Be still and stay bright.
It's come to tell you
There's something not right.

Something you're missing,
You are ignoring it too.
It's sending a message
From cosmos to you.

Go watch the movie
Called *Dr Strange.*
You never will see
Your sickness the same.

Don't be fearful, cross,
Angry or cold.
This sickness has come
To help you evolve.

Healing is a matter of time, but it is sometimes also a matter of opportunity.
– Hippocrates

What's Your Poison ?

Alcohol, it will change
The way you behave.
You don't see it. We do.
We try to be brave.

You can't see the change,
But your family sure can.
You're moody, you're grumpy.
Think you're more of a man?

Booze dulls the mind,
Takes us way below.
We're more like animals;
We reap what we sow.

It's one big seduction
This alcohol thing;
Beer, wine or spirits
Will not happiness bring.

You can't do anything
Without beer in your hand!
Whether family picnic or
Playing cricket on the sand.

Young people they think
Their youth will be lost
If they don't party hard
And get totally sloshed.

Ask the doctors and cops
What they think of booze.
Accidents, bashings;
It's horrible news.

A film star for breakfast
Drank daily six-pack of beer.
He became really mean.
Lost his whole career.

Head-ons in cars,
Falling from a height,
Bashing your family;
Oh my, what a fright.

Go see the movie
Manchester by the Sea.
What drink and drugs did
Led to such misery.

Our culture says okay
To have a few drinks.
Go down that road often, and
You may stand on the brink.

I have known some people
Who have lost their lives.
The booze made them careless;
It said, *I love you.* It lies.

Drink makes us say words
That we'll one day regret.
I've said things to people
I just cannot forget.

I once went without it
For more than a year.
I felt light and clean,
And with nothing to fear.

At my cousin's wedding
I did not drink a drop.
Did not say mean words
Or not know when to stop.

Alcohol says, *Come on,*
You know you want more!
But the very next day
Your head is so sore.

You feel so disgusting.
You're wiped out. You're trashed.
You swear never again
Will you get that smashed.

But our memory forgets,
And in a week or two
You've made up with alcohol;
You're back drinking like new.

One night in a pub fight,
A bloke knocks you over.
There's blood on your face;
That sure makes you sober.

Other drugs are taboo,
But alcohol is worse;
Sold on every corner.
It's our culture's curse.

You can live without it
And **be** content too.
Say goodbye to the Drink;
You will feel brand new.

Are you stressed and anxious?
Think the answer's in Drink?
Check the app *Calm;*
Brings you back from the brink.

It's cheaper and cleaner
Than a bottle of booze.
Your life will get better;
You now get to choose.

Ann Dowsett Johnston
Wrote a great book called *Drink.*
From the top to the gutter
Is where she did sink.

A problem? Oh no!
That's what she thought.
Tried to hide it from others.
The Drink had her caught.

Creeps up on you slowly;
One drink becomes two,
Then three become four.
What's happening to you?

Have you learned your lesson?
No, probably not.
Will take a disaster.
You've sure lost the plot.

How 'bout your kids?
Now they've started drinking.
You become the observer;
See how many they're sinking.

They've watched you for years;
They see who you are.
Can't start preaching now;
Too much time at the bar.

Take a break from the booze.
Hello Sunday Morning;
The name of a website;
Awareness is dawning.

Your relationship with drink,
Can you bear the sight?
Take a long, hard look.
May give you a fright.

Pretends to be a friend,
But it really is a foe.
Hurts your body and mind;
Down the black hole you go.

Say, *No* at the party,
Say, *No* at the lunch,
Say, *No* at the wedding,
Say, *No* as you munch.

You'll feel clean and alert
As your body does heal.
Let go of the alcohol;
You'll **be** amazed how you feel!

Yes, you can do this.
Think when you were a child.
You lived life without it.
You played and you smiled!

You don't need the booze
To **be** who you are.
You're now more authentic;
Relax. You've come far.

That's all drugs and alcohol do, they cut off your emotions in the end.
– Ringo Starr

The Pain-Body

Heard of the pain-body
To which Eckhart refers?
Gets sucked into drama
And gets on your nerves.

If your partner is having
A bit of a spat,
Your pain-body is drawn in,
Won't leave it at that.

When you did this and
When you did that,
I don't like it, and
You should take it all back.

Just a thought of the past
Can bring it alive.
Takes over completely;
It will start to drive.

Thoughts of the past
Take on some momentum.
They get bigger and bigger.
You start to invent them.

So, how do you stop
This body of pain,
Which loves to take over
To see what it will gain?

You become present.
Yes, that's what you do.
Stop the thoughts in your head
And know they're not you.

As you put a stop
To the anger and fear,
The pain-body subsides
And can't live when you're here.

So the next time
Your partner carries on in a fuss,
Don't react with a comeback,
And try not to cuss.

Say to yourself,
Their pain-body is active.
Just remain silent
And **be** slightly passive.

The pain-body won't like that.
It's in for a fight.
But with calm, quiet presence,
There's no need to bite.

You pretend that your partner
Is a possessed kind of demon.
They won't listen to sense,
And you just cannot reason.

Your pain-body too gets
Drawn into the drama,
And this is why couples
Start to wear armour.

Be aware, **be** alert.
The pain-body lurks
Inside every human
Who's ever been hurt.

Be still and **be** kind.
Just listen with care.
Soon it will pass
So please don't despair.

The pain-body is clever;
It must have its way,
But if you don't feed it,
It has nowhere to stay.

It loves to feel hurt,
Righteous and mean.
But if you stay present,
It cannot get seen.

We all have a pain-body
That lives deep inside,
Triggered by jealousy,
Plus anger and pride.

Look out for it now,
And don't get drawn in.
The pain-body is dormant
When you're present within.

Be the change you want to see happen.
– Arleen Lorrance

Racism

You walk out your door
And you know what's ahead:
The stares and the whispers
That you've started to dread.

Your religion says
That your hair not be seen,
But the place where you live
Thinks this is obscene.

It's like you are wearing
A sign on your head
That says, *Pick on me please.*
Think I'll stay in bed.

As I walk along
People point, people stare.
They don't see my face,
Just my hijab, no hair.

As I sit down to eat
At the local café,
I can feel their eyes,
Their whispers. I pray:

Please God, let these humans
See my heart and my light.
I am a Muslim.
Please, end my plight.

Sometimes they're not whispers;
It's loud words that curse.
They say hurtful mean things.
It can't get much worse.

Standing out in the crowd,
It does get me down.
I just want to be me,
Not a freak. Not a clown.

There's a wall in their mind
That they have built.
Race, skin, religion
Tends to put them off kilt.

It's called Islamophobia,
And some people excel
At reacting with hatred.
In ignorance we dwell.

You were born here,
I was born there.
We're all human beings.
There's no need to despair.

You are not *better*,
And you are not *worse*.
To have thoughts like this
Makes life a curse.

What would it be like
To **be** just like the rest?
My hair flowing free,
They'd no longer see *pest*.

Then they might know me,
They'd accept who I am,
Now they can't do that,
Their judgements they ram.

The worst thing is about
My faith they know nought.
Nor do they want to;
They see extremists. Distraught.

If we judge the religion,
The face or the clothes,
Can't connect with others.
There's no chance to evolve.

So next time you see me
On the street or café,
Let your heart speak to mine.
We'll connect; that's the way.

Our true nationality is mankind.
– H.G. Wells

Embarrassment

Do you get embarrassed
By what your partner says?
When you're out with friends
He dismisses your pres.

Perhaps he's too quiet,
And doesn't say boo.
Or maybe she flirts,
And that annoys you.

Does she make jokes that
Inside make you cringe
Or take over the meal
So you cannot impinge?

Our partners are teachers.
So what are they for?
May not make us happy,
But more conscious, for sure.

We have this idea
Of how they should **be**.
When they don't live up,
We're embarrassed, aren't we?

Why do they do this?
Why do they say that?
Our mind starts to churn,
And we're in for a spat.

If someone hit you
With a pole or a stick,
Getting angry with it,
Well, you'd feel like a twit.

That's what it's like when
Your partner acts so.
They're not their real self,
It's their ego you know.

It's best just to feel that
They are separate soul.
Detach yourself now;
Don't play the role.

For they can't behave
As we want them to.
Drop expectations and
You'll feel better, not blue.

You don't want the fights
That come after the meal.
When you speak your mind,
You lose your appeal.

You might have a word
When the moment has passed.
State your case gently.
They may listen at last.

Be gentle and kind.
Forgive how they act.
It's just who they are.
Not fiction. It's fact.

Know you can't change them.
Do you think you will?
Accept who they are.
Be the space and be still.

When you don't resist
Their outward show,
You'll be more relaxed;
Your spirit will glow.

Remember they're teachers.
They're guiding you to
A more awake being;
A better version of you.

Be like the night to cover others' faults.
– Rumi

Someone Who Bugs You

Is there someone you know
Who makes you see red?
They say things that hurt you,
An ache in the head.

It's easy to get angry
And push them away.
To see them as enemy
And dislike them all day.

This person's a teacher
If you just see it right.
Be still, and **be** present.
And try not to bite.

There's something they say
That triggers a switch.
In your head or your heart.
Just **be** and feel which.

Instead of reacting
To the words and the deeds,
Breathe in and breathe out
And see where that leads.

Be still and just know
That the ego's at work.
Taken over your friend.
The ego is a jerk.

If you get upset
And say something mean,
Your ego says, *Gotcha!*
Hee, hee, I've been seen!

The ego in us
Is our foe, not our friend.
Likes to make enemies
And see friendships end.

See through the cruel words,
And look for the light
That shines through us all,
If we only have sight.

So next time you meet up
With that person who's mean,
Look for their kindness,
And let it **be** seen.

You'll notice a change,
Believe me, you will.
You'll feel so much better.
Be present and still.

Try to be a rainbow in someone's cloud.
– Maya Angelou

The Ego

Have you heard of the ego?
It really is sly.
It hides in your body,
A bit like a spy.

It pretends to protect you
And make you feel swell,
By saying you're the best
And separate as well.

It's all about ME where
The ego's concerned.
It says you're most special,
Clever and learned.

It puffs up with pride
When it buys something new,
But it can get annoyed
If you purchase it too.

It tells you it's YOU
That matter the most.
Forget all the rest,
May as well be a ghost.

Your opinion it thinks
Is definitely best;
You have to be right,
And here comes the test.

Someone tells you you're wrong.
You say, *How do you dare!*
The ego gets ruffled
By even a hair.

So next time the ego says
That you're number one,
That you're the ants pants
And worth a great sum,

Look around at the others,
The people you know.
Everyone in the world
Is just like your bro'.

We're all the same really;
There is no *you* and *me*.
Like drops in the rivers,
The lakes and the sea.

Their skin may be different,
Their religion as well,
But see through to their essence
And then you can tell,

That we're all family,
Us humans. We are.
The ego's not right.
No, you're not the star.

Be humble and kind
To the others you meet.
See them as you, and
Then you will be sweet.

Tell the ego to go
Take a jump in the lake.
It wants you to listen,
But you tell ego it's fake.

See the others as you.
You just can't go wrong.
You'll feel more connected,
Joyful and strong.

People may forget what you said – but they will never forget how you made them feel.
– Carl Buehner

Suffering

A tummy ache, a headache
Or you just feel plain blue.
You know what it's like
When it all gets to you.

You can't seem to shift it,
It just won't go away.
You're praying the pain
Is not here to stay.

Well, here's what you do
When that pain in your head
Has you grumble and groan,
Makes you go back to bed.

Sense your whole body.
Feel the presence of **now**.
The suffering's a story.
Don't give it power.

Gaze at a flower,
A bird or a tree.
Leave the story behind,
And simply just **be**.

The pain, it will go
If you don't feed the thoughts.
Just stop the chatter,
And you'll not get caught.

Next time you notice
You're not feeling so great,
Stop the thinking.
Just **be**. It's never too late.

That voice in the head can
Make things seem so bad.
Something that happened,
Causes us to feel sad.

Say, **no** to the thinking,
The sad story and more.
Come back to The Now.
Feel your essence, your core.

Never to suffer would never to have been blessed.
– Edgar Allan Poe

jencompton.com

Your Smart Phone

One day you'll be old,
But your kids won't forget
How you made them feel
When with you, I'll bet.

Remember *I see you*
In the *Avatar* movie?
Look past their faults and
Help them feel groovy.

Kids don't hear the words;
They see who you are.
The way you behave
Is what sets the bar.

If you complain about
Everything under the sun,
Their sense of joy weakens
And they'll have less fun.

If you criticise
Every move that they make,
They'll start to withdraw
For fear of mistake.

Look at yourself well, and
Ask yourself this:
Am I good company
Or off like fish?

Do I moan? Do I shout?
Spend too much time with my phone?
Do I ignore my kids?
Say, *Just leave me alone!*

All of these moments are
Like drops in a bucket.
Each drop makes a life,
So try not to stuff it.

Gaze at your kids like
You look at your phone.
Interest and wonder,
You'll notice they've grown.

You go to a café,
And sit down to eat.
If you take out your phone,
Their eyes you'll not meet.

They long to connect;
To talk during the meal.
Look at them really;
You'll see how they feel.

Stop stressing about
All the stuff you're to do.
Stay in this moment;
Your kids will love you.

Be kind to your kids.
Watch out for that stress;
Can make you feel grumpy.
Life gets a big mess.

Take some time every day
To enjoy and just **be**.
The phone and the iPad,
Not important, you'll see.

The years fly by quickly,
And kids grow so fast.
Take care of this moment,
'Cause it soon will be past.

Give kids the space to
Talk, ask and **be**.
Stay positive and kind.
They'll remember you see.

Not what you said but
The respect that was shown.
Being present with them
Instead of your phone.

They know with the phone
They cannot compete, but if
You turn it to silent,
You give them a great treat.

Make kids feel like you have
All the time in the world.
They should grab your attention
Like a beautiful pearl.

Your kids they will judge
The job that you've done.
Be kind and **be** present.
Then the future you've won.

We are all so much together, but we are all dying of loneliness.
– Albert Schweitzer

Death

Death it is certain.
Yes, it will come.
Wherever you go.
From it, you can't run.

It comes to us all,
But when we know not.
Each day think of this fact,
Against it don't plot.

In bed, on the road,
In a plane or a boat,
In a building, a house,
Urban or remote.

You could be quite young
Or an adult and healthy.
You may be sick and old,
Could be poor or wealthy.

Heart disease or cancer,
Diabetes, old age,
So many conditions
Remove us from life's page.

When the moment arrives,
It can be quite scary;
Mind separates from body.
We must all be wary.

Not always fearful,
Just intensely aware.
Death may come this moment.
I don't mean to scare.

So, this is why we must
Seize each moment **now**.
Be joyful and grateful.
Come on, make a vow.

Your *life* is really
A series of moments.
On your deathbed the mind
Best have grateful component.

The state of your mind
On your deathbed is great.
Thoughts that are kind and forgiving
Will determine your fate.

A mind that is gentle,
Calm and at ease
Helps your next rebirth,
And from suffering frees.

The reason we must work
On a much kinder mind
Is 'cause it determines where
Ourselves we will find.

When the time of death comes,
Be calm and not scared.
Rejoice in your life.
Be pleased how you fared.

Think of people you've known
And of all beings on earth.
Kind thoughts towards others
Will get you good rebirth.

As you take your last breath now,
Chest goes up and then down,
Fill your mind with compassion
For all others around.

Death is not the opposite of life, but a part of it.
– Haruki Murakami

Intimacy

There once was a woman
Who felt sad in her heart.
She so longed to talk,
But he'd have no part.

They had lived together
For many long years,
What she wanted to hear
Did not reach her ears.

He'd talk about news,
Work, his health, bank loan,
But personal matters
Was a *no-go* zone.

It felt so insane;
The intimate partner,
Would not allow her speech.
No way could she barter.

When she tried to tell him
What was in her heart,
He'd just roll his eyes
Or get up with a start.

There was never the space;
Permission to **be**.
She so longed to express
Herself and feel free.

Have you ever felt this
With your dad or your mum?
Conversation you want
That just doesn't come.

You so long to tell them
The stuff in your heart,
But they talk about school
Or what's in the shopping cart.

So what can we do
When this state of affairs
Has us feeling wretched,
So full of despair?

You could send an email
With what's in your heart.
It's not really perfect,
But at least it's a start.

They can't interrupt,
Get angry or shout.
You can express then;
Say what it's all about.

You may get a reply,
But then you may not.
At least you've spoken;
You've emptied the pot.

A walk in nature
Together is good.
Their heart may relax,
You'll **be** understood.

People are frightened
Of opening the heart,
But avoiding what's there
Is not very smart.

What starts to happen is
The heart gets smothered,
Like a diamond with
Dirt that is covered.

They feel so afraid
Of what it may reveal.
They avoid *personal*;
Their life is not real.

The people who loved them
All start to give up.
Years. No intimacy;
So empty their cup.

Don't be afraid **now**
To open your heart.
Just surrender all;
It's where you must start.

If you cover it up,
Your relations aren't true.
People you live with,
They cannot know you.

They'll play the game and
May buy you presents,
But what they ache for is to
Connect with your essence.

For it is in giving that we receive.
– Saint Francis of Assisi

Your Opinion

Some state their opinion
As if it's the truth.
They get all caught up.
You need to be a sleuth.

They're only happy
If you so agree
With their take on things.
It's the little me.

They make their statement
As if it's a fact.
You nod and you smile.
You cannot back-chat.

It's no good talking
For they cannot hear.
Anything that you say,
Goes out through one ear.

It doesn't take long
To work out this type.
You quickly catch on.
You're careful, polite.

The more we identify
With our thoughts,
The more we do not listen;
In our head, we are caught.

It really is sad
To get stuck in a groove.
Only see your side;
You will not be moved.

So, what can you do to
Not fall into this trap?
Not listen to others?
Not fill in the gap?

Treat your opinions
Like food at a buffet.
Pick up and put down;
Keep them separate, away.

Don't hold them too tight;
Light as a feather,
'Cause they are just concepts
Like terms used for weather.

Don't let your opinions
Get fixed in concrete.
Because if you do,
You'll put people to sleep.

Others long to be seen,
To have their thoughts heard.
Without the attack,
Which you have preferred.

Watch your opinion like
A cloud in the sky.
That's soft and empty
As it passes by.

Try debating sometime
From the opposite view.
This other perspective
Will be good for you.

Just try to take interest
In what others do say.
Listen so well.
Repeat back, okay?

If the words from your
Mouth you think are wise,
But you don't hear others,
They will you despise.

They might give a nod,
Pretend to agree,
But deep down inside
They long to **be** free.

State what you will,
As you are able,
With calm and with presence,
Not thumping the table.

Your ego loves opinion.
It wants to be right,
But your message is weak
If you shout, get uptight.

What starts to happen,
Although you can't see,
Is that the person who's there
Loses their right to **be**.

Their personality
Starts to diminish,
Because they can't talk.
You won't let them finish!

Very soon they give up.
It's useless trying.
They just have to pretend
To agree with your whining.

Relationships suffer
When you think you're right.
You can't see others
Who sit there in fright.

Give them their space,
Let them **be** free.
If you don't listen,
Their soul you'll not see.

Let go of opinions
Like releasing a kite.
As hard as it is,
It will feel so right.

If they disagree,
Rejoice in that fact.
You'll learn something new.
You can make a pact:

Don't get mean if their
Thoughts aren't just like yours.
Be aware, **be** awake.
Be quiet and pause.

So now you know
Your life-long mission.
People feel safe when you
Respect their position.

Give them the space
To express and to state.
Be silent and listen.
Your opinion can wait.

The greatest deception men suffer is from their own opinions.
– Leonardo da Vinci

Habits

The plane touches down.
We're alive and we're safe.
But instead of rejoicing,
We complain without grace.

An amazing feat of
Engineering and skill.
A miracle really and
Yet we're blind to it still.

There was a baby screaming
And a man who was loud,
But we miss the point really.
Instead of sky we see cloud.

Complaining and moaning
Start small; nothing much
But soon become a habit,
All you see, all you touch.

Such a sin, such a pity
To live life this way.
Not the path I choose,
I vow with dismay.

Every day I see close
How I don't want to live.
I choose *amazing life,* and
Rejoice in what is.

Half empty or half full?
It's your choice how you see.
Get rid of self-centredness.
Yes, from it you must flee.

You think it's corny?
You think it's not cool, but
If you're grateful for what is,
Then you're smart, not a fool.

It makes such a difference
When you vow *not to complain.*
You feel more at ease.
Your mind is now sane.

It is what it is.
Accept. Open. **Be** glad.
If you don't live like this
You and others get sad.

Three cheers for the pilots!
Three cheers for the crew!
They were skillful and kind.
Were you grateful? Were you?

At first, it may be hard.
You need to rewire your brain.
But you'll feel so much lighter
When you vow not to complain.

Take baby steps first.
Try to catch yourself often.
Your thoughts, emotions and words –
Will all start to soften.

Little by little,
You'll feel lighter and free
As you say, *Thank you for this.*
Those around you agree.

Change your perception, your mind,
Your mood and your face
As you give thanks for what is.
You'll live life with more grace.

At first, it is hard, but
With practise you'll see
That not moaning about stuff
Keeps you glad, sets you free.

Be thankful and stop complaining.
– anonymous

Books that have changed me

Just like you, I can't possibly list *all* the books that have impacted me in my life, but here are some of my favourites. I haven't included fiction. Listed below are the non-fiction books I just cannot part with because they are a joyful reminder of the mind-body transformation over the years. A heartfelt thank you to all the authors of these jewels and their insights and also to the authors that I haven't been able to list here but who have helped to mould me into the person I am today and will be tomorrow.

****

Bienkowski, Andrew and Akers, Mary. *Radical Gratitude: and Other Life Lessons Learned in Siberia.* Sydney: Inspired Living, 2008.

Byrne, Rhonda. *The Secret.* New York: Atria Books, 2006.

Byron, Katie. *Loving What is: Four Questions That Can Change Your Life.* London: Rider, 2002.

Chopra, Deepak. *Ageless Body, Timeless Mind: A Practical Alternative to Growing Old.* London: Rider, 1993.

Chopra, Deepak. *The Seven Spiritual Laws of Success: A Practical Guide to the Fulfilment of Your Dreams.* Sydney: Random House, 2001.

Dalai Lama, H. H. the, *How to Practise: The Way to a Meaningful Life.* London: Rider, 1988.

Dalai Lama, H. H. the, *The Meaning of Life: Buddhist Perspectives on Cause and Effect.* Somerville: Wisdom Publications, 2000.

Dalai Lama, H. H. Tenzin Gyatso, the Fourteenth. *How to See Yourself As You Really Are: A Practical Guide to Self-Knowledge.* New York: Atria Books, 2007.

Dalai Lama, H. H. the, and Thubten Chodron. *Approaching the Buddhist Path.* Somerville: Wisdom Publications, 2017.

Dalai Lama, H.H. the, and Franz Alt. *Our Only Home: A Climate Appeal to the World*. Munich: Benevento Publishing, 2020.

Dass, Ram & Bush, Mirabai. *Walking Each Other Home: Conversations on Loving and Dying*. Colorado: Sounds True, 2018.

Emoto, Masaru. *The True Power of Water: Healing and Discovering Ourselves*. Hillsboro: Beyond Words Publishing, 2003.

Epstein, Mark. *Advice Not Given: A Guide to Getting Over Yourself*. New York: Penguin Press, 2018.

Frankl, Viktor E. *Man's Search for Meaning: The Classic Tribute to Hope from the Holocaust*. London: Rider, 2004.

Gawain, Shakti. *Creative Visualisation: Use the Power of Your Imagination to Create What You Want in Your Life*. San Rafael: New World Library, 1978.

Gawande, Atul. *Being Mortal: Medicine and What Matters in the End*. New York: Picador/Macmillan, 2015.

Harari, Yuval Noah. *Sapiens: A Brief History of Humankind*. Israel: Dvir Publishing House Ltd, 2014.

Harris, Russ. *The Happiness Trap: Based on ACT: A Revolutionary Mindfulness-based Programme for Overcoming Stress, Anxiety and Depresssion*. London: Constable & Robinson Ltd, 2008.

Hawkes, Tim. *boy oh boy: how to raise and educate boys*. Sydney: Pearson Education Australia, 2001.

Hawkins, David R. *Power VS Force: The Hidden Determinants of Human Behavior*. Sydney: Hay House, 1998.

Kalanithi, Paul. *When Breath Becomes Air*. New York: Random House, 2016.

Ladner, Lorne. *The Lost Art of Compassion: Discovering the Practice of Happiness in the Meeting of Buddhism and Psychology*. New York: Harper Collins, 2004.

Leimbach, Claire, McShane, Trypheyna and Virago, Zenith. *The Intimacy of Death and Dying: Simple Guidance to Help You Through.* Sydney: Inspired Living, 2009.

Loden, Geshe Acharya Thubten. *Meditations on the Path to Enlightenment.* Melbourne: Tushita Publications, 2005.

Michie, David. *Buddhism for Busy People: Finding Happiness in an Uncertain World.* Sydney: Inspired Living, 2004.

Myss, Caroline. *Invisible Acts of Power: Personal Choices That Create Miracles.* New York: Free Press, 2004.

Nhat Hanh, Thich. *Being Peace.* Berkeley: Parallax Press, 2005.

Peck, M. Scott. *The Road Less Travelled: A New Psychology of Love, Traditional Values and Spiritual Growth.* London: Rider, 1987.

Ricard, Matthieu. *Happiness: A Guide to Developing Life's Most Important Skill.* London: Atlantic Books, 2007.

Rumi. *The Big Red Book: The Great Masterpiece Celebrating Mystical Love & Friendship.* New York: Coleman Barks, 2011.

Shantideva. *A Guide to the Bodhisattava's Way of Life.* Dharamsala: Library of Tibetan Works and Archives, 2012.

Sogyal Rinpoche. *The Tibetan Book of Living and Dying.* New York: Ebury Publishing, 1992.

Tegchok, Geshe Jampa. *Transforming Adversity into Joy and Courage: An Explanation of the Thirty-Seven Practices of Bodhisattvas.* New York: Snow Lion, 1999.

Tegchok, Geshe Jampa. *The Kindness of Others: A Commentary on the Seven-Point Mind Training.* Weston: Lama Yeshe Wisdom Archive, 2006.

Tenzin Palmo. *Reflections on a Mountain Lake: A Western Nun Talks on Practical Buddhism.* Sydney: Allen & Unwin, 2002.

Tolle, Eckhart. *The Power of Now: A Guide to Spiritual Enlightenment.* Sydney: Hodder, 2004.

Tolle, Eckhart. *A New Earth: Awakening to Your Life's Purpose*. New York: Penguin, 2005.

Tuttle, Will. *The World Peace Diet: Eating for Spiritual Health and Social Harmony*. New York: Lantern Books, 2005.

Yeshe, Lama Thubten. *Becoming Your Own Therapist and Making Your Mind an Ocean: An Introduction to the Buddhist Way of Thought*. Boston: Lama Yeshe Wisdom Archive, 2007.

Zopa Rinpoche, Lama Thubten. *How Things Exist: Teachings on Emptiness*. Boston: Lama Yeshe Wisdom Archive, 2008.

Zopa Rinpoche, Lama Thubten. *Wholesome Fear: Transforming Your Anxiety about Impermanence & Death*. Boston: Wisdom Publications, 2010.

HEALTH

Beyer, K.A. *The Lemon Detox Diet Program: Rejuvenation Sensation*. Grantham: PNP Ltd, 2020.

Bredesen, Dale E. *The End of Alzheimer's Program: The First Protocol to Enhance Cognition and Reverse Decline at Any Age*. New York: Avery, 2020.

Chopra, Deepak. *Perfect Health: The Complete Mind Body Guide*. London: Bantam Books, 2000.

Davis, William. *Wheat Belly*. New York: Rodale, 2011.

Doidge, Norman. *The Brain That Changes Itself: Stories of Personal Triumph from the Frontiers of Brain Science*. New York: Penguin Books, 2007.

Dowsett Johnston, Ann. *Drink: The Intimate Relationship Between Women and Alcohol*. Sydney: HarperCollins, 2013.

Gillespie, David. *Why Sugar Makes Us Fat*. Melbourne: Penguin Group, 2008.

Gundry, Steven R. *The Plant Paradox: The Hidden Dangers in Healthy Foods That Cause Disease*. New York: HarperCollins, 2017.

Gundry, Steven R. *The Longevity Paradox: How to Die Young at a Ripe Old Age.* New York: HarperCollins, 2019.

Gundry, Steven R. *The Energy Paradox: What to Do When Your Get-Up-And-Go Has Got up and Gone.* New York: HarperCollins, 2021.

Holford, Patrick. *The Optimum Nutrition Bible.* London: Piatkus, 1997.

Holford, Patrick. *The 10 Secrets of Healthy Ageing: How to Live Longer, Look Younger and Feel Great.* London: Piatkus, 2012.

Holfrod, Patrick. *The Alzheimer's Prevention Plan: 10 Proven Ways to Stop Memory Decline and Reduce the Risk of Alzheimer's.* London: Piatkus, 2014.

Jockers, David. *Keto Metabolic Breakthrough: A Radical Approach to Reversing Metabolic Dysfunction.* Las Vegas: Victory Belt Publishing, 2020.

Mosconi, Lisa. *The XX Brain: The Groundbreaking Approach for Women to Prevent Dementia and Alzheimer's Disease and Improve Brain Health.* Sydney: Allen & Unwin, 2020.

Osborne, Peter. *No Grain, No Pain: A 30-day diet for eliminating the root cause of chronic pain.* Carlton: Nero, 2016.

Stevenson, Shawn. *Eat Smarter: Use the Power of Food to Reboot Your Metabolism, Upgrade your Brain and Transform your Life.* New York: Hachette Book Group, 2020.

Wilson, Sarah. *I Quit Sugar: Your Complete 8-Week Detox Program and Cookbook.* Sydney: Macmillan, 2013.

Reflections

Hello again friend, I hope you can relate to the poems in *Life's a Mango* and I invite you to return to them again and again. May they inspire you to let your heart **be** heard. If some of the content arouses deep emotions for you, consider contacting your local help line.

When we regularly jot down our thoughts/stories/poems or reflections, they can help us to connect with our higher self and to see situations with more wisdom and clarity. This is what I've found over the years.

Each of us has untapped hidden treasures which long to express themselves through us. Whatever form that expression takes for you; whether it's writing, gardening, dancing, drawing or some other form of artistic expression, you will feel a greater sense of connection with yourself, with others and with life.

Life's a Mango has taken me on an inner journey that constantly keeps evolving. When I write poems about life, I give myself permission to both express what has been lying dormant in my heart for years as well as what moves me now, in the present moment.

What does your heart long to share? May this book inspire you to find your voice.

Be gentle. **Be** authentic. **Be** brave. **Be** you.

Love,

Jen

Every day I'm reminded by others how I want to live this life and how I do not.
– Jen Compton

Genuine happiness cannot
be defined by material
and sensual satisfactions,
but only by mental
and spiritual development
that always
acknowledges others
and their needs.

His Holiness the Dalai Lama

Mandalas

These mandalas are here for you to colour
and enjoy. Colour them as you reflect on
the rhyming wisdom or relax your mind.

Let your light shine, and
Let others' shine too.
We're all connected;
There's no *me* and no *you*.